T'an Ssu-t'ung:
An Annotated Bibliography

Institute of Chinese Studies
The Chinese University of Hong Kong
Bibliography and Index Series (3)

T'an Ssu-t'ung:
An Annotated Bibliography

Chan Sin-wai

The Chinese University Press
Hong Kong

International Standard Book Number: 962-201-210-8

The Chinese University Press
The Chinese University of Hong Kong
SHATIN, N.T., HONG KONG

Typesetting by The Chinese University Press
Printing by Union Printing Company

CONTENTS

CONTENTS

PREFACE

For more than five years, I have been engaged in the study of T'an Ssu-t'ung. Like so many other students of modern Chinese intellectual history, I am fascinated by his heroic deeds and his illuminating work, the *Jen-hsüeh*. When I began my research work earlier last year in the Institute of Chinese Studies in The Chinese University of Hong Kong, the idea of annotating extant works on T'an Ssu-t'ung began to take shape. After a period spent in collecting materials, during which I paid a visit to England for that purpose, the idea has now finally translated itself into reality.

The present study contains more than 200 items, consisting of articles, books and theses by or on T'an Ssu-t'ung, written either in Chinese or English between 1878 and 1978. For each item, I have tried to describe its contents, the source materials used, and original contributions made, if any. For T'an's original works listed here, a detailed description of their contents is provided in order that readers who have no access to them can at least have some idea of what is contained. I have not rated the secondary sources with asterisks because any such judgment is bound, I think, to be too subjective. Readers who are interested in the scholarship on T'an Ssu-t'ung may well find useful the Introduction section of my forthcoming translation of the *Jen-hsüeh*. For some works at present unavailable to me, I have regrettably to leave their annotation until some time in the future when there is need for a revised edition of this work.

I should like to take this opportunity to express the intellectual debts I owe to several of my teachers. I must thank Professor Wang Teh-chao, who, during my undergraduate years at The Chinese University, initiated me into the field of Chinese intellectual history, and after the completion of my Ph.D. at the University of London, guided me onto further research in specific problems in the field of modern Chinese history. I should also like to express my sincere gratitude to my mentor at the School of Oriental and African Studies, Dr. Charles Curwen, for his guidance in my graduate work and for his care and kindness through the years. Professor D. C. Lau, formerly of London University and currently professor of Chinese at The Chinese University, has benefitted me with his encyclopaedic knowledge of Chinese culture and his meticulous correction of my translation. Finally, I must express my gratitude to Dr. Raymond Lorantas, formerly head of the History Department of Chung Chi College, The Chinese University of Hong Kong, and currently Professor of History at Drexel University, for his unconditional assistance in both academic and other matters throughout all these years.

In preparing this work for publication, I have been helped by several persons. I am greatly indebted to Professor Ch'en Ching-ho, the Director of the Institute of Chinese Studies, who is the main architect in bringing this work to print; to Professors Wang Teh-chao and D. C. Lau again for proofreading it; to Mr. Wang Erh-min, senior lecturer in the History Department of The Chinese University, for helping me to collect articles from Taiwan and for furnishing me with two theses done directly or indirectly under him; to my friend Mr. Kam Pak-ho for his assistance in the preparation of the Appendix; and to Mr. William C. C. Ho of the Chinese University Press for his meticulous editing.

Lastly, I would like to dedicate this book, with all my affections, to my parents, brothers and sisters, wife Lai-lin, and newborn son Kai-ho.

Institute of Chinese Studies   S. W. Chan
The Chinese University of Hong Kong
March 1979

ANNOTATED BIBLIOGRAPHY

001 **Chan Sin-wai** 陳善偉 , **"The Buddhist Theme in Late Ch'ing Political Thought: 1890-1911, with Special Reference to T'an Ssu-t'ung"**
Unpublished Ph.D. thesis, School of Oriental and African Studies, University of London, 1977. 387 pages.

This study explores the religious, cultural and political significance of Buddhism in the late Ch'ing intellectual world through an examination of the writings of influential figures like Liang Ch'i-ch'ao 梁啓超 , K'ang Yu-wei 康有爲 , Chang Ping-lin 章炳麟 , and particularly T'an Ssu-t'ung. It is believed that Buddhism came to play a part in these reformers' thought because of several factors: the rekindled interest in Buddhism brought about by Layman Yang Wen-hui 楊文會, the need to find a counterweight to Christianity, the search for a new unifying ideology for China as Confucianism crumbled before the challenge from the West, and the immense potentiality of Buddhism to satisfy the intellectuals' diverse cultural and political needs. The Buddhist thought of T'an Ssu-t'ung is examined in chapters 3, 4, and 5. It is shown here that the application of Buddhism in late Ch'ing political thought was generally utilitarian in purpose. Buddhism not only served as the all-embracing philosophy in T'an's eclectic synthesis in the *Jen-hsüeh* 仁學 , but also furnished a foundation for the major concepts in the treatise and was closely related to his radical thinking. To T'an and other like-minded Buddhist intellectuals, Buddhism was neither world-abnegating nor pessimistic, but indigenous, this-worldly and altruistic. As their writings show, Buddhism could be used to invalidate Christianity, to suggest that science and Western philosophy had their roots in Chinese cultural tradition, to provide unity of thought, cultivate revolutionary character, uplift morality and dismantle deep-seated erroneous concepts and parochial views.

002 **Chan Sin-wai** 陳善偉 , **"Liang Ch'i-ch'ao: A Biography of T'an Ssu-t'ung"**
(Included in the translator's forthcoming work, *An Exposition of Benevolence: The Jen-hsüeh of T'an Ssu-t'ung, A Translation with An Introduction*)

This is a close (as opposed to an elegant) English translation of the most quoted biography of T'an. Fully annotated with discussion of dubious points.

1

003 **Chan Sin-wai** 陳善偉 , **"Wan-Ch'ing fo-hsüeh yü cheng-chih kai-ke— lüeh-lun T'an Ssu-t'ung te fo-hsüeh ssu-hsiang"** 晚清佛學與政治改革 ── 略論譚嗣同的佛學思想 [**Buddhism and political reforms in late Ch'ing—a brief discussion on the Buddhist thought of T'an Ssu-t'ung**]
In *Hua-ch'iao jih-pao* 華僑日報 (Hong Kong), 10th June, 1974.

A study of the historical background (the Buddhist revival in modern China), personal factors (his chequered childhood etc.) and his affiliation with Buddhist converts, that led T'an to embrace Buddhism. The author believes that Buddhism was the most influential school in the formulation of T'an's major concepts. Doctrines of the Wei-shih 唯識 School were freely used to show that Buddhism was analogous to Confucianism, Western science and other disciplines.

004 **Chan, Wing-tsit** 陳榮捷 (**tr. & comp.**), *A Source Book in Chinese Philosophy*
Princeton: Princeton University Press, 1963, pp. 737-742.

In this book, the chapter (Chapter 40) on T'an Ssu-t'ung is entitled "The Philosophy of Humanity (*Jen*) in T'an Ssu-t'ung". Some parts of the *Jen-hsüeh* are translated here which include the subjects of "Ether and humanity", "The principle of nature and human desires", "Neither production nor extinction" and "Daily renovation". The compiler gives brief comments on the selections. The translations sometimes closely follow Derk Bodde's rendering of Fung Yu-lan's *A History of Chinese Philosophy* (1953). Basically, the compiler believes that T'an is a replica of K'ang Yu-wei on a small scale, or, in other words, an elaborator and modifier of K'ang's basic philosophy of humanity. T'an is regarded as "the only one in Chinese history to have devoted a whole book to *jen.*" The compiler also says that T'an's ideas of *jen* are significant in two respects: he regards *jen* as reality and he identifies *jen* with Ether.

005 **Chang Ch'i-chih** 張豈之 *Chung-kuo che-hsüeh shih-lüeh* 中國哲學史略 [**A concise history of Chinese philosophy**]
Shensi: Jen-min ch'u-pan-she, 1974, pp. 240-245.

A brief account of T'an's thought.

006 **Chang Ch'i-chih** 張豈之 , **"T'an Ssu-t'ung che-hsüeh ssu-hsiang te chi-ke wen-t'i"** 譚嗣同哲學思想的幾個問題 [**Several problems in T'an Ssu-t'ung's philosophy**]
In Hou Wai-lu 侯外廬 (ed.), *Wu-hsü pien-fa liu-shih chou-nien chi-nien*

chi 戊戌變法六十週年紀念集 [A commemorative volume on the six-tieth anniversary of the 1898 Reform Movement]. Peking: K'o-hsüeh ch'u-pan-she, 1958, pp. 43-58.

Originally published under the title "Tui T'an Ssu-t'ung che-hsüeh ssu-hsiang te chi-tien k'an-fa" 對譚嗣同哲學思想的幾點看法 [Several viewpoints regarding the philosophical thought of T'an Ssu-t'ung], *Jen-wen tsa-chih* 人文雜誌, Vol. 3 (Aug. 1957), pp. 39-46.

The author explains how T'an's philosophical thought was related to his political ideas and why such a radical thinker as T'an was idealistic in his *Weltanschauung*. He believes that K'ang Yu-wei's conception of *jen* 仁 shaped T'an's idea of *jen*. *Jen* in T'an's thought is the source of the universe and the highest authority. It is given the feature of *t'ung* 通, which, when applied to the social and economic realms, means *laissez-faire*, equality and the need to reform. *Jen* is also used to extirpate the deep-seated feudal concepts and Confucian ethics of *san-kang wu-lun* 三綱五倫 (the three bonds and five relationships). Ether is pantheis-tic. The *Jen-hsüeh* is idealistic but has materialistic minglings. This is because T'an was keen to accept the practical use of Western science but lacked a proper understanding of it. Often he garbled scientific concepts so as to suit his idealistic frame of thinking. His ideal society is a capitalistic one. In sum, T'an's thought is full of contradictions. It is idealistic, pantheistic, agnostic and relativistic. This can be ascribed to several factors: (1) T'an was a patriot who strongly advocated reform but was unable to see the force of the masses. He thus sought remedy in mental power; (2) T'an had the general tendencies of a New Text scholar —fanciful and whimsical, making some wild analogies; (3) Christian books exerted considerable influence on T'an, and he was thus inclined to draw erroneous analogies between theology and science.

007 **Chang Lei-fu** 張磊夫, **"P'ing-lun T'an Ssu-t'ung te cheng-chih ching-chi ssu-hsiang"** 評論譚嗣同的政治經濟思想 **[On the political and economic thought of T'an Ssu-t'ung]**

In *Ch'un-ch'iu* 春秋, Vol. 13, No. 1 (July 1970), pp. 15-16.

The author says that T'an's philosophy was grounded on the idea that "when *tao* 道 changes, *ch'i* 器 should also change accordingly." In his political thinking, T'an advocated reform, the overthrow of the Manchus and the abolition of autocracy. He championed democracy, and his political ideal was the Great Unity. His political views were rather extraordinary in that he suggested regional self-government and

3

thought that if a country was ill-managed, order could only be restored by aggravating her deterioration. In keeping with his basic philosophical stance, T'an's economic thought emphasized: (1) *t'ung*, which meant the promotion of international trade; (2) dynamism, which gave rise to the idea of efficiently opening up China's rich resources; and (3) extravagance.

008 **Chang Li-wen** 張立文 , **"Lun T'an Ssu-t'ung 'Jen-hsüeh' che-hsüeh te wei-hsin chu-i shih-chih"** 論譚嗣同仁學哲學的唯心主義實質 **[On the idealistic nature of the philosophy expressed in T'an Ssu-t'ung's** *Jen-hsüeh*]

In *Chiang-han hsüeh-pao* 江漢學報 , Vol. 6 (June 1964), pp. 49-57.

Also collected in Chou K'ang-hsieh 周康燮 (ed.), *Chung-kuo chin san-pai-nien hsüeh-shu ssu-hsiang lun-chi erh-pien* 中國近三百年學術思想論集二編   [Second collection of articles on Chinese learning and thought of the last three hundred years] . Hong Kong: Ch'ung-wen shu-tien, 1974, pp. 157-165.

This article joins the materialist-or-idealist debate on the thought of T'an and criticizes all supposedly wrong interpretations of the major philosophical concepts in the *Jen-hsüeh*—such as those of Fung Yu-lan 馮友蘭 , Hsü I-chün 徐義君 and P'ang P'u 龐朴 . According to the author, *jen* is equivalent to "mind" and "consciousness". *T'ung*, which generates equality and unity, is the most fundamental meaning of *jen*. Ether, mental power and external forms are synonyms used according to the context. The author concludes that (1) T'an's thought is idealistic; (2) this is because he was conditioned by his limited social contacts and scientific knowledge; (3) T'an's economic ideas are capitalistic; and (4) he was a radical reformer.

The author also criticizes Chang Te-chün 張德鈞 for relating the development of T'an's philosophy to his political ideas, and for saying that T'an was a revolutionary, not a reformer.

009 **Chang Te-chün** 張德鈞 , **"Liang Ch'i-ch'ao chi T'an Ssu-t'ung shih shih-shih pien"** 梁啓超記譚嗣同事失實辨 **[Clearing up the inaccuracies in Liang Ch'i-ch'ao's biography of T'an Ssu-t'ung]**

In *Wen-shih* 文史 , Vol. 1 (Oct. 1962), pp. 81-85.

Also collected in Chou K'ang-hsieh 周康燮 (ed.), *Chung-kuo chin san-pai-nien hsüeh-shu ssu-hsiang lun-chi erh-pien*   中國近三百年學術思想論集二編 [Second collection of articles on Chinese learning and thought of the last three hundred years]. Hong Kong: Ch'ung-wen shu-tien, 1974, pp. 243-248.

This article is devoted to proving some inaccuracies in Liang's "T'an Ssu-t'ung chuan". According to the author, Liang's account of T'an's being unable to meet K'ang Yu-wei in Peking is untenable. He quotes from Liang's *Yin-ping-shih wen-chi* 飲冰室文集 [Collected writings of the Ice-drinking Studio] and his "San-shih tzu-shu" 三十自述 [Reflections at the age of thirty] according to which Liang came to know T'an through the introduction of Wu T'ieh-ch'ao 吳鐵樵 whom Liang met only in 1896. T'an in 1895 was in Hupeh while K'ang was in Peking. If T'an had gone to Peking in the summer of that year, he could have met K'ang. So Liang must have made a mistake in his dating. The author also examines T'an's attitude towards K'ang and the Society for the Study of National Strengthening and concludes that Liang's account is again dubious. According to the author, K'ang came to know T'an by name before the latter had even heard of K'ang. It was only through Liang that T'an came to know of K'ang's ideas. The author maintains that T'an apparently did not meet Liang until 1896 and that at no time was T'an a slavish disciple of K'ang.

Criticizes also some mistakes in the presentation of facts and dates by Yang T'ing-fu 楊廷福 and T'ang Chih-chün 湯志鈞.

010 **Chang Te-chün** 張德鈞, **"T'an Ssu-t'ung ssu-hsiang shu-p'ing"** 譚嗣同思想述評 [**An interpretative account of the thought of T'an Ssu-t'ung**] In *Li-shih yen-chiu* 歷史研究, Vol. 3 (1962), pp. 27-60.

A very detailed examination of the development of T'an's thought through different stages. The author believes that it grew from materialism to idealism and from reformism to democraticism. Before the age of twenty-six, T'an was an "ethnocentricist", as can be patently detected in his work "Chih yen" 治言 [Views on state management]. Between twenty-six and thirty, T'an studied under Ou-yang Chung-ku 歐陽中鵠 and became a fervent admirer of Chang Tsai 張載 and Wang Fu-chih 王夫之. With his newly acquired knowledge of Western science, he began to compare Chinese and Western sciences. When the author examines T'an's representative work in this period, "Shih-chü ying lu pi-chih" 石菊影廬筆識, he believes that T'an at that time was preoccupied with Wang Fu-chih's idea of mónistic *ch'i* 器, and was strongly opposed to any kind of religion and superstition. Shocked by China's disastrous defeat in the Sino-Japanese War, T'an decided to make an

5

abrupt change in both his intellectual and political outlook. This can be seen from his two letters, "Shang Ou-yang Pan-chiang shih shu erh— hsing suan-hsüeh i" 上歐陽瓣薑師書二—興算學議 and "Ssu-wei i-yün t'ai tuan-shu—pao Pei Yüan-cheng" 思緯壹壺臺短書—報貝元徵 . From these two letters, it can be seen that T'an advocated regional govern- ment and was resentful of the Manchus' reckless signing away of rights and territories to foreign powers. He applied Wang Fu-chih's *tao-ch'i* 道器 ideas to advocate reform. At the age of thirty-two, T'an was com- pletely under the influence of Buddhism. An examination of the nature of the major concepts and the structure of the *Jen-hsüeh* reveals that T'an's thought can only be subjective idealism. The author thinks that T'an should more appropriately be regarded as a revolutionary rather than a reformer. However, T'an was ignorant of the machinations of the foreign powers and had some misconceptions about them.

Criticizes Yang T'ing-fu 楊廷福, T'ang Chih-chün 湯志鈞, Fung Yu- lan 馮友蘭 .

Criticized by Chang Li-wen 張立文 .

011 **Chang T'ieh-chün** 張鐵君, **"Hu-nan ssu-hsiang-chieh te i hui-hsing—T'an Liu-yang"** 湖南思想界的一彗星—譚瀏陽 **[A meteor of the intellectual world of Hunan, T'an Ssu-t'ung of Liuyang]**
      In *Hu-nan wen-hsien* 湖南文獻 , Vols. 6 & 7 (Oct. 1972), pp. 119-121.

A highly panegyric, seemingly interpretative, brief introduction to the thought of T'an. The author argues that many Western concepts— a notable example being Ether—now being dismantled by Western scientists, remained valid in T'an's thought because T'an had remoulded them in his own way; therefore they can stand the test of time.

012 **Chang Yü-t'ien** 張玉田 , **"Lun T'an Ssu-t'ung che-hsüeh ssu-hsiang te wei-hsin chu-i hsing-chih—yü Yang Cheng-tien t'ung-chih t'ao-lun kuan-yü T'an Ssu-t'ung te che-hsüeh wen-t'i"** 論譚嗣同哲學思想的唯心主義 性質—與楊正典同志討論關於譚嗣同的哲學問題 **[On the idealistic nature of the philosophical thought of T'an Ssu-t'ung—A discussion with Comrade Yang Cheng-tien on the problems relating to the philo- sophy of T'an Ssu-t'ung]**
      In *Kuang-ming jih-pao* 光明日報 , 16th May, 1956.

The author criticizes Yang's materialistic interpretation of T'an's thought. He argues that, first, by T'an's own definition, Ether is clearly idealistic. Second, the idealistic Buddhist doctrines had great influence on the formation of T'an's major concepts. Third, Wang Fu-chih's idea that *tao* 道 is inseparable from *ch'i* 器, albeit materialistic, is scarcely seen in the *Jen-hsüeh*; it is rather an idea that T'an fancied in 1895. Fourth, the ideas of "non-creation and non-destruction", "one is inclusive of many" and the like are all Buddhist doctrines. Finally, T'an's epistemology is idealistic, and he emphasized the importance of transforming consciousness into wisdom.

013 **Chang Yüan-chi** 張元濟 **(ed.),** ***Wu-hsü liu chün-tzu i-chi*** 戊戌六君子遺集 **[Posthumous collection of the writings of the six martyrs of the *coup d'etat* of 1898]**
Shanghai: Shang-wu yin-shu-kuan, 1917.

This consists of six volumes in a set. Vols. 1 & 2 reproduce T'an Ssu-t'ung's "Tung-hai Ch'ien-ming-shih san-shih i-ch'ien chiu-hsüeh ssu-chung" 東海褰冥氏三十以前舊學四種. Vol. 1 is "Liao-t'ien i-ko wen" 寥天一閣文, which is in two *chüan* 卷, totalling forty *p'ien* 篇. Vol. 2 is "Mang-ts'ang-ts'ang chai shih" 莽蒼蒼齋詩, "Yüan-i-t'ang chi wai wen ch'u-pien" 遠遺堂集外文初編 and "Yüan-i-t'ang chi wai wen hsü-pien" 遠遺堂集外文續編.

014 **Chao Ching** 趙靖, **"T'an Ssu-t'ung te ching-chi ssu-hsiang"** 譚嗣同的經濟思想 **[The economic thought of T'an Ssu-t'ung]**
In *Pei-ching ta-hsüeh hsüeh-pao* 北京大學學報, Vol. 1 (Feb. 1963), pp. 21-28.

A well-written article which deals with an important but often neglected aspect of T'an's thought. The author describes in detail the economic ideas of the martyr, whom he considers far more radical than his peers.

015 **Chao Erh-hsü** 趙爾巽, **K'o Shan-min** 柯劭忞 *et al.* **(ed. & comp.),** ***Ch'ing-shih kao*** 清史稿 **[Draft history of the Ch'ing dynasty]**
Originally published in 1927. Reprinted in Hong Kong: Hsiang-kang wen-hsüeh yen-chiu-she, 1960, p. 1423.

This brief biography of about 450 words is included in *chüan* 251 of the "lieh-chuan" 列傳 (collected biographies) section. It is almost a paraphrased version of Liang's "T'an Ssu-t'ung chuan" except in noting that (1) T'an had hard feelings towards his father and (2) T'an and his friend T'ang Ts'ai-ch'ang 唐才常 were known as "Liu-yang erh-sheng" 瀏陽二生 because of their excellent performance in the Hunan-Hupeh Academy.

7

016 **Chen Fu** 振甫 , **"Ts'ung Liang Ch'i-ch'ao t'an tao T'an Ssu-t'ung chuan"**
     從梁啟超談到譚嗣同傳 [**A discussion of Liang Ch'i-ch'ao and his bio-**
     graphy of T'an Ssu-t'ung]
     In *Yü-wen hsüeh-hsi* 語文學習 , Vol. 11 (Nov. 1957), pp. 33-36.

     Describes Liang's literary skill and introduces the character of T'an.

017 **Ch'en Chang** 陳彰 , **"T'an Ssu-t'ung yü Ta-tao Wang Wu"** 譚嗣同與大刀
     王五 [**T'an Ssu-t'ung and Great Sword Wang Wu**]
     In *Ch'ang-liu* 暢流 , Vol. 35, No. 7 (May 1967), p. 12.

     Describes the well-known swordsman Wang Wu by quoting at length
     the five-character verse by Yang Yün-shih 楊雲史 . The author also
     describes how the relationship between T'an and Wang Wu developed.

018 **Ch'en Ching-chih** 陳敬之 , **"T'an Ssu-t'ung"** 譚嗣同 [**T'an Ssu-t'ung**]
     In *Ch'ang-liu* 暢流 , Vol. 27, No. 12 (Aug. 1963), pp. 8-12; Vol. 28,
     No. 4 (Oct. 1963), pp. 7-10.

     The main source of this article is Yang I-feng's 楊一峯 "T'an Ssu-
     t'ung". As such, it bears close resemblance to Yang's ideas and presen-
     tation. It discusses T'an's character, thought, scholarship, literary style,
     poetry and the gap between his theory and practice. The author main-
     tains that T'an died for the cause of reform and not for the Emperor,
     and that T'an's literary style before the age of thirty was predominantly
     of the euphuistical antithetic style of the 6th and 7th cneturies. After
     the age of thirty, T'an often wrote in the eight-legged style. When T'an
     later studied the "New Learning", his style changed significantly and be-
     came what the author called "the new literary form of T'an Ssu-t'ung"
     which contributed much to the emergence of the "literary reform" of
     the early Republican period. The author also believes that T'an's acts
     were in keeping with his words.

019 **Ch'en Ching-chih** 陳敬之 , **"T'an Ssu-t'ung te hsing-hsing, chih-chieh, ssu-**
     hsiang ho hsüeh-shu" 譚嗣同的性行、志節、思想和學術[**The character,**
     personality, thought and learning of T'an Ssu-t'ung]
     In *Hu-nan wen-hsien* 湖南文獻 , Vol. 4, No. 1 (Jan. 1976), pp. 20-27.

     A reprint of the above article. The contents of these two articles are
     identical except (1) the subtitle of the second paragraph is rewritten as
     "以學行仁，以身殉道" ; (2) the only note referring to Yang I-feng has
     been deleted.

020 Ch'en Ching-chih 陳敬之 , "Wei hsien-cheng erh hsi-sheng te liang-ke
     Hu-nan ying-han—t'an T'an Ssu-t'ung ho Sung Chiao-jen" 為憲政而犧
     牲的兩個湖南硬漢—— 談譚嗣同和宋教仁 [Two courageous Hunanese
     who sacrificed their lives for the cause of constitutional government—a
     discussion of T'an Ssu-t'ung and Sung Chiao-jen]
         In *I wen chih* 藝文誌 , Vol. 4 (Jan. 1966), pp. 23-26.

     This article examines the common factors which led to the martyrdom
     of T'an Ssu-t'ung and Sung Chiao-jen.

021 Ch'en Chu-chia 陳諸家 , "T'an Ssu-t'ung shih wei-wu chu-i che ma?—
     chieh-shao kuan-yü T'an Ssu-t'ung che-hsüeh ssu-hsiang te cheng-lun"
     譚嗣同是唯物主義者嗎?——介紹關于譚嗣同哲學思想的爭論   [Was
     T'an Ssu-t'ung a materialist?—an introduction to the debate on the
     philosophical thought of T'an Ssu-t'ung]
         In *Pei-ching jih-pao* 北京日報 , 11th January, 1957, p. 3.

     A general survey of the materialist-or-idealist debate about T'an. The
     author takes no stance himself.

022 Ch'en Hsü-lu 陳旭麓 , "Lun T'an Ssu-t'ung te min-chu chu-i ssu-hsiang
     yü kai-liang chu-i cheng-chih shih-chien te mao-tun" 論譚嗣同的民主主
     義思想與改良主義政治實踐的矛盾 [On the contradiction between T'an
     Ssu-t'ung's democratism and reformism in political practice]
         In *Hsüeh-shu yüeh-k'an* 學術月刊 , Vol. 1 (Jan. 1958), pp. 59-68.

     The author sums up the political and social ideas of T'an under three
     main heads: (1) democratic thinking; (2) opposition to all feudal ethics
     and scholarship; and (3) opposition to Manchu rule. T'an's economic
     thought also had three main features: (1) the favouring of capitalistic
     extravagance over frugality; (2) the levelling of the rich and the poor;
     (3) the tapping of natural resources with the use of machines. The
     author believes that T'an's thought was revolutionary but his political
     practice was reformist, reflecting the transitional status of the class of
     which T'an was a representative. His belief in Buddhism also made him
     a soul lost between materialism and idealism.

023 Ch'en Nai-ch'ien 陳乃乾, "Liu-yang T'an hsien-sheng nien-p'u" 瀏陽譚先
     生年譜 [A chronological biography of Mr. T'an Ssu-t'ung of Liu-yang]
         In *T'an Liu-yang ch'üan-chi* 譚瀏陽全集 [Collected works of T'an
     Ssu-t'ung of Liu-yang]. Shanghai: Wen-ming ch'u-pan-she, 1952,
     pp. 11-27.

A fairly unembellished chronological biography of T'an. It is drawn almost entirely from T'an's "San-shih tzu-chi" 三十自紀 for the years before the age of thirty. After that, it merely reproduces Liang's biography. A disappointing piece of work.

024 **Ch'en Po-ta** 陳伯達 , **"Lun ch'i-meng ssu-hsiang chia T'an Ssu-t'ung"** 論啟蒙思想家譚嗣同 **[On the enlightenment thinker T'an Ssu-t'ung]**
    In *Chen-li te chui-ch'iu hsü-p'ien* 眞理的追求續篇 [A sequel to the pursuit of truth] . Shanghai: Sheng-huo shu-tien, 1939, pp. 163-220.

    This article is identical to the following one. The title had been changed to the above to suit, presumably, the subtitle of the above book, which is《新啟蒙運動史論文二集》 [Essays on the history of the New Enlightenment, vol. 2] .

025 **Ch'en Po-ta** 陳伯達 , *Lun T'an Ssu-t'ung* 論譚嗣同 **[On T'an Ssu-t'ung]**
    Peking: Jen-wen yin-wu-she, 1934. 118 pages.

    This is the first work which touches on the issue of whether T'an was an idealist or a materialist. Despite its brevity, this book is frequently quoted by Marxist historians, particularly the author's assessment of T'an's role in modern Chinese intellectual thought. It is Marxist-oriented, and often gives background descriptions of the events in T'an's period. The author quotes extensively from Marxist classics to substantiate his view that T'an was a materialist, though idealistic elements were not lacking in his thought. Because of the author's prominent position in the political hierarchy of Communist China before his fall, the article has had enormous influence both on the interpretation of T'an's thought and on his role in modern China.
    The book begins with a description of the historical background which drove T'an to the idea of reform. In discussing the content of the *Jen-hsüeh*, the author thinks that T'an took from Chinese traditional thought the idea of *jen* and from Western science the concept of Ether. They are equivalent and are the ultimate source and reality. They are, however, not prime movers of the universe in the sense that "God" is in the West, but they coexist with all creation. Soul and body are separated in T'an's thinking. Soul, which is equivalent to *jen* and Ether, is valued while the body is belittled. This creates internal contradictions in his philosophy. Buddhism and Taoism play an important role in the formulation of T'an's thought. T'an was the first to scrutinize Chinese cultural traditions systematically. When the thought of T'an is compared with

that of K'ang Yu-wei, it turns out that they are closely connected. The author concludes that T'an's contribution lies in his criticism of the old feudal China, which not only left an indelible mark on the 1898 Reform Movement, but also gave the 1911 Revolution a spiritual weapon, paving the way for the May Fourth Movement.

026 Ch'en Tan-nung 陳丹農 , "Lüeh-t'an T'an Ssu-t'ung shih" 略談譚嗣同詩 [A brief discussion of the poems of T'an Ssu-t'ung]
     In *Wen-hsüeh i-ch'an tseng-k'an* 文學遺產增刊 , Vol. 12 (Feb. 1963), pp. 154-164.

027 Cheng Ho-sheng 鄭鶴聲 , "Lun T'an Ssu-t'ung pien-fa ssu-hsiang chi ch'i li-shih i-i" 論譚嗣同變法思想及其歷史意義 [On T'an Ssu-t'ung's ideas on reform and their historical significance]
     In *Wen shih che* 文史哲 , Vol. 9 (Sept. 1954), pp. 41-48.

     The author discusses T'an's critical views on feudalism, his radical ideas and his nationalism. He thinks that T'an failed to become a revolutionary because of his very strong idealistic thinking.
     Criticized by Tung Ni 冬尼 .

028 Chi Lu K'e 冀魯客 , "T'an Ssu-t'ung yü T'ai-wan" 譚嗣同與台灣 [T'an Ssu-t'ung and Taiwan]
     In *Chung-yang jih-pao* 中央日報 , 6th June, 1958, p. 6.

029 Ch'i Wei-kuo 齊衛國 , "Tui T'an Ssu-t'ung yü-chung-shih te li-ts'e" 對譚嗣同獄中詩的蠡測 [Conjecturing the prison-poem of T'an Ssu-t'ung]
     In *I wen chih* 藝文誌 , Vol. 83 (Aug. 1972), pp. 57-58.

     This article deals with the allusion in T'an's last poem.

030 Chiang Wei-ch'iao 蔣維喬 , *Chung-kuo chin san-pai-nien che-hsüeh shih* 中國近三百年哲學史 [History of Chinese philosophy of the last three hundred years]
     Shanghai: Chung-hua shu-chu, 1932, pp. 117-122.

     A brief biographical account and an introduction to T'an's ideas in the *Jen-hsüeh*.

031 Ch'ien Mu 錢穆 , "T'an Ssu-t'ung te Jen-hsüeh" 譚嗣同的仁學 [The *Jen hsüeh* of T'an Ssu-t'ung]
     In Pao Tsun-p'eng 包遵彭 *et al.* (ed.), *Chung-kuo chin-tai-shih lun-*

11

ts'ung 中國近代史論叢 [Collection of articles on modern Chinese history]. Taipei: Cheng-chung shu-chu, 1970, Vol. 7, pp. 138-147.

Originally published as part of the author's article entitled "K'ang Yu-wei hsüeh-shu shu-p'ing" 康有爲學術述評 [A critical account of the learning of K'ang Yu-wei], in *Ch'ing-hua hsüeh-pao* 清華學報, Vol. 11, No. 3 (July 1936), pp. 583-656.

Later included as part of Chapter 14 of the author's *Chung-kuo chin san-pai-nien hsüeh-shu shih* 中國近三百年學術史 [An intellectual history of China during the last three hundred years]. Shanghai: Ta-hsüeh ts'ung-shu, 1937, Vol. 2, pp. 667-678.

Though brief, this piece of writing invites much discussion. The author compares the *Jen-hsüeh* to Huang Tsung-hsi's 黃宗羲 *Ming-i tai-fang lu* 明夷待訪錄 and to K'ang Yu-wei's *Ta-t'ung shu* 大同書 and concludes that the *Jen-hsüeh* is simply an elaboration of the ideas propounded in the *Ta-t'ung shu.* The author maintains that T'an's martyrdom was not in keeping with his idea that people should not die for the emperor. If T'an had fled to Japan, the author argues, he could still have the chance of becoming someone like Ch'en She 陳涉 or Yang Hsüan-kan 楊玄感 and plan for the future. But T'an died for the Emperor, an act which was rather meaningless.

Criticized by Hou Wai-lu 侯外廬, Hsiao Jen-ying 蕭人英 and others.

032 **Chien Po-tsan** 翦伯贊 *et al.* **(ed. & comp.),** *Wu-hsü pien-fa* 戊戌變法 **[Historical materials on the 1898 Reform Movement]**
Shanghai: Shen-chou kuo-kuang she, 1953, 4 vols.

This is the eighth series of the *Chung-kuo chin-tai-shih tzu-liao ts'ung-k'an* 中國近代史資料叢刊 edited by Chung-kuo shih-hsüeh-hui 中國史學會. Vol. 2 contains excerpts of several letters of T'an Ssu-t'ung (pp. 559-569). Vol. 3 reprints T'an's "Chih-shih p'ien" 治事篇 (pp. 83-92). Vol. 4 contains excerpts from Ch'en Nai-ch'ien's chronological biography (pp. 179-181) and an article by Ch'en Shu-t'ung 陳叔通 《譚嗣同就義與梁啟超出亡》(pp. 329-330) and poems selected from 《秋雨年華之館叢脞書》(pp. 348-349). At the end of Vol. 4, Chien Po-tsan has an annotated bibliography of the 1898 Reform Movement in which some works on T'an are included; see particularly pp. 599-601 and 613.

033 **Chih Fei** 知非, **"T'an Ssu-t'ung yü Wu-hsü pien-fa"** 譚嗣同與戊戌變法 **[T'an Ssu-t'ung and the Reform Movement of 1898]**

In *Jen-min jih-pao* 人民日報 , 21st May, 1958, p. 8.

Briefly outlines the life of T'an.

034 Chin Liang 金梁 (ed.), *Chin-shih jen-wu chih* 近世人物誌 [Notes on contemporary figures]
Taipei: Kuo-min ch'u-pan-she, 1955, pp. 353-354.

Contains only a few lines from Weng T'ung-ho 翁同龢 to describe the character of T'an.

035 Ching An 景安 , "Liang Jen-kung yü T'an Ssu-t'ung te chiao-i" 梁任公
與譚嗣同的交誼 [The friendship between Liang Ch'i-ch'iao and T'an Ssu-t'ung]
In *Hu-nan wen-hsien* 湖南文獻 ,Vol. 6, No. 1 (Jan. 1978), pp. 27-30.

Identical to the following entry.

036 Ching An 景安 , "Liang Jen-kung yü T'an Ssu-t'ung te chiao-i" 梁任公
與譚嗣同的交誼 [The friendship between Liang Ch'i-ch'iao and T'an Ssu-t'ung]
In *Tsai-sheng* 再生 , Vol. 20 (Mar. 1973), pp. 13-15.

Describes in terse, lucid style how the friendship between T'an and Liang began and ripened during 1896-1898.

037 Chou Jung-hsiang 周榕祥 , "T'an Ssu-t'ung chiu-i ch'ien-hou" 譚嗣同
就義前後 [T'an Ssu-t'ung before and after martyrdom]
In *Tung-nan hua-pao* 東南畫報 , Vol. 55 (7th Sept., 1958).

038 Chou K'ang-hsieh 周康燮 , "Shu T'an Ssu-t'ung chien chuan shu Wen Hsin-kuo kung Chiao-yü ch'in chi chen-chi hou" 書譚嗣同兼撰書文信國
公蕉雨琴記眞蹟後[Epilogue to T'an Ssu-t'ung's authentic autograph of "An Account of the revered Wen Tien-hsiang's Chiao-yü lute"]
In *Chung-kuo chin san-pai-nien hsüeh-shu ssu-hsiang lun-chi erh-pien*
中國近三百年學術思想論集二編 [Second collection of articles on Chinese learning and thought of the last three hundred years] . Hong Kong: Ch'ung-wen shu-tien, 1971, p. 249.

The author is himself the owner of this authentic scroll of T'an's calligraphy. He describes its size and discusses the date it was written.

039 Chou Shih-fu 周世輔, "Lun T'an Ssu-t'ung te cheng-chih ssu-hsiang" 論譚嗣同的政治思想 [On the political thought of T'an Ssu-t'ung]
In *Sheng-li yüeh-k'an* 生力月刊, Vol. 5, No. 50 (Dec. 1971), pp. 12-13.

The author sums up the main features of T'an's political thought as follows: (1) his objection to foreign rule; (2) his dislike of autocracy and accordingly the teachings of Hsün-tzu which advocated it; (3) his proposal for reform and his conceptualization of the Great Unity wherein lies no national boundaries.

040 Chou Shih-fu 周世輔, "Lun T'an Ssu-t'ung te jen-hsing lun, jen-sheng kuan yü chih-hsing lun" 論譚嗣同的人性論、人生觀與知行論 [On T'an Ssu-t'ung's ideas on human nature, life and the relationship between theory and practice]
In *Sheng-li yüeh-k'an* 生力月刊, Vol. 5, No. 52 (Feb. 1972), pp. 23-24.

T'an followed Wang An-shih 王安石 in asserting that it was necessary to conform to human nature and desires. He also followed Tai Chen 戴震 in maintaining that human desires, like human nature, are good. And deriving mainly from Ch'eng Hao 程顥, T'an believed that things and the self, Heaven and all sentient beings, and others and the self, are one. His martyrdom can be ascribed to his belief in non-creation and non-destruction of all sentient beings. Of theory and practice, T'an evidently placed greater importance on the former.

041 Chou Shih-fu 周世輔, "Lun T'an Ssu-t'ung te tao-te kuan" 論譚嗣同的道德觀 [On the moral views of T'an Ssu-t'ung]
In *Sheng-li yüeh-k'an* 生力月刊, Vol. 5, No. 53 (Mar. 1972), pp. 27-28.

The author explains that *jen* in T'an's thought is inclusive of wisdom, courage and knowledge. T'an wanted to "burst through all enmeshing webs" 衝決網羅 and he was strongly opposed to the Confucian "three bonds and five relationships". On the issue of sex, T'an believed that the idea of sex as obscene ought to be done away with. Sex education was needed to achieve this purpose. Prostitutes, moreover, should be licensed.

042 Chou Shih-fu 周世輔, "Lun T'an Ssu-t'ung te yü-chou che-hsüeh" 論譚嗣同的宇宙哲學 [On the cosmology of T'an Ssu-t'ung]
In *Sheng-li yüeh-k'an* 生力月刊, Vol. 5, No. 51 (Dec. 1971), pp. 11-12.

The author believes that *jen* is idealistic because it is an idea drawn from Wei-shih 唯識 Buddhism. Ether is employed to explain mental power. *Jen* is absolute, impartial, pervasive, uncreated and imperishable. In human beings, *jen* is mental power, soul and the spring of wisdom; in the universe, *jen* is Ether, electricity and the source of all creation. T'an also held that everything has senses. His ideas of non-creation and non-destruction sprang from Buddhism and Taoism.

043 **Chou Shih-fu** 周世輔 , **"T'an Ssu-t'ung hsien-sheng te che-hsüeh ssu-hsiang kai-shu"** 譚嗣同先生的哲學思想概述 **[An outline of the philosophical thought of Mr. T'an Ssu-t'ung]**
      In *Hu-nan wen-hsien* 湖南文獻 ,Vol. 7, No. 3 (1969-1970), pp. 16-17.

      A brief discussion of T'an's views on human nature, life and his epistemology.

044 **Chou Shih-fu** 周世輔 , **"T'an Ssu-t'ung hsien-sheng te yü-chou lun"** 譚嗣同先生的宇宙論 **[The cosmological views of Mr. T'an Ssu-t'ung]**
      In *Hu-nan wen-hsien* 湖南文獻 , Vol. 4, No. 4 (Oct. 1976), pp. 5-7.

      Identical to the previous article.

045 **Ch'ou T'ung** 仇同 , **"T'an Ssu-t'ung hsien-sheng chuan-lüeh"** 譚嗣同先生傳略 **[A brief biography of Mr. T'an Ssu-t'ung]**
      In *Ch'ang-liu* 暢流 , Vol. 25, No. 11 (July 1962), p. 12.

      The author, a colleague of T'an Ssu-t'ung's adopted grandson T'an Hsün-ts'ung 譚訓聰 , from whom he often heard anecdotes about T'an, wrote this short article to express his admiration for the heroic acts of the martyr. Yet, despite the author's close relationship with T'an's grandson, this piece of writing is almost a mere reproduction of Liang's biography.

046 **Chu Jui-k'ai** 祝瑞開 , **"Lun T'an Ssu-t'ung"** 論譚嗣同 **[On T'an Ssu-t'ung]**
      In Hou Wai-lu 侯外廬 (ed.), *Wu-hsü pien-fa liu-shih chou-nien chi-nien chi* 戊戌變法六十週年紀念集 [A commemorative volume of the sixtieth anniversary of the 1898 Reform Movement] . Peking: K'o-hsüeh ch'u-pan-she, 1958, pp. 23-42.

      Discusses the historical background of T'an Ssu-t'ung's period, his philosophy, and his social and political ideas. The author asserts that T'an was an idealist and explains how idealistic elements mingled with materialistic ones in T'an's thought.

15

047 **Chüeh Shui Chai chu-jen** 覺睡齋主人 **(comp.),** *Hsiang-pao lei tsuan* 湘報類纂 **[Classified compilation of articles from the** *Hunan Daily* **]**
Reprinted in Taipei: Ta-t'ung shu-chu, 1969.

A complete set of the *Hunan Daily* is not readily accessible to historians outside Mainland China. T'an, as an editor of this paper, contributed voluminously to it. The compiler of this volume makes available some of T'an's writings here.

048 **Chung-kuo k'o-hsüeh-yüan che-hsüeh yen-chiu-so Chung kuo che-hsüeh shih tsu** 中國科學院哲學研究所中國哲學史組 **(ed.),** *Chung-kuo che-hsüeh shih tzu-liao hsüan-chi—chin-tai chih pu* 中國哲學史資料選輯── 近代之部 **[Selected materials on the history of Chinese philosophy—The modern period]**
Peking: Chung-hua shu-chu, 1959, Vol. 6, pp. 292-356.

Selected here are sections from Part 1 of the *Jen-hsüeh* and 《思緯壹壹臺短書── 報貝元徵》, both with explanations and very detailed annotations.

049 **Chung-kuo k'o-hsüeh-yüan che-hsüeh yen-chiu-so Chung-kuo che-hsüeh shih tsu** 中國科學院哲學研究所中國哲學史組 **and Pei-ching ta-hsüeh che-hsüeh hsi Chung-kuo che-hsüeh shih chiao-yen shih** 北京大學哲學系中國哲學史教研室 **(ed.),** *Chung-kuo li-tai che-hsüeh wen-hsüan* 中國歷代哲學文選 **[Selected sources on philosophies of the various dynasties of China]**, *Ch'ing-tai chin-tai pien* 清代近代編 **[The Ch'ing and modern periods]**
Peking: Chung-hua shu-chu, 1963, Vol. 2, pp. 285-336.

The selected sections from Part 1 of the *Jen-hsüeh* in the above entry are reprinted here with only minor changes in annotation. There is an introduction on the life and thought of T'an. The editors believe that T'an was a materialist.

050 **Fei Hui-ch'ang** 費會昌, **"T'an Ssu-t'ung hsien-sheng te shih ch'iu chieh"** 譚嗣同先生的詩求解 **[Tentative interpretation of a poem by Mr. T'an Ssu-t'ung]**
In *Hsing-shih* 醒獅 , Vol. 6, No. 6 (June 1968), p. 23.

051 **Fung Yu-lan** 馮友蘭 , *Chung-kuo che-hsüeh shih* 中國哲學史 **[A history of Chinese philosophy]**

Shanghai: Shang-wu shu-chu, 1934, pp. 1021-1030.

Translated into English by Derk Bodde as Fung Yu-lan, *A History of Chinese Philosophy*, Princeton: Princeton University Press, 1952, Vol. 2, pp. 691-705.

The author believes that T'an's idea of *jen* was derived from Western science and from the sayings of Wang Shou-jen 王守仁 and Ch'eng Hao 程顥 : "The man of *jen* takes Heaven earth and the myriad things as one." *Jen* is the function of Ether. The concept of Ether being neither created nor destroyed was drawn from Chang Tsai's 張載 statement that "When *ch'i* 器 condenses, its visibility becomes apparent so that there are then the shapes of individual things."

052 **Fung Yu-lan** 馮友蘭 , **"Lun T'an Ssu-t'ung"** 論譚嗣同 **[On T'an Ssu-t'ung]**
In *Wen-hui pao* 文滙報 , 13th & 14th September, 1961.

Later collected in Fung Yu-lan, *Chung-kuo che-hsüeh shih lun-wen ch'u-chi* 中國哲學史論文初集 [First collection of articles on the history of Chinese philosophy]. Shanghai: Jen-min ch'u-pan-she, 1962, pp. 430-454.

The author considers T'an as a materialist. T'an regards the materialistic Western concept Ether as the idea of *ch'i* 器 in the thought of Chang Tsai 張載 and Wang Fu-chih 王夫之 . The concept of non-creation and non-destruction, however, had its origin in Buddhism. Although Ether cannot be created or destroyed, the things it composes are subject to creation and destruction, which T'an describes with the idea of "invisible creation and destruction" 微生滅 or "lesser transmigration" 細輪迴 . Mental power is the spiritual form of Ether. T'an describes it in terms of eighteen kinds of dynamic forces and it is therefore materialistic. Ether, electricity and mental power are one. Ether and electricity are the materialistic aspects and mental power the spiritual aspect. The author believes that one fundamental tendency of T'an was to use the material phenomena to explain the spiritual ones. This tendency was materialistic. The author also discusses T'an's historical views, which were capitalistic and utopian. He believes that T'an's thought was radical but was not sufficiently radical to transcend K'ang Yu-wei's reformist frame of thinking.

053 **Han Jui** 涵銳 **and Chiang Feng** 江鋒 , **"T'an Ssu-t'ung te Mang-ts'ang-ts'ang chai"** 譚嗣同的莽蒼蒼齋 **[The Mang-ts'ang-ts'ang Studio of T'an Ssu-t'ung]**

17

In *Pei-ching jih-pao* 北京日報, 2nd June, 1957.

Tells us what the couplets hanging in T'an's studio actually said.

054 **Ho Kan-chih** 何幹之, ***Chung-kuo ch'i-meng yün-tung shih*** 中國啟蒙運動
史[**A history of the enlightenment movement in China**]
Shanghai: Sheng-huo shu-tien, 1947, pp. 63-76.

In his 14-page discussion of T'an's character and thought, the author
includes the conversation between T'an and Yüan Shih-k'ai 袁世凱 in
order to compare their contrasting characters. Basically, he believes that
T'an was a materialist (or neo-materialist), but mechanistic and con-
ceptual in other aspects.

055 **Hou Wai-lu** 侯外廬, ***Chin-tai Chung-kuo ssu-hsiang hsüeh-shuo shih*** 近代
中國思想學說史 [**A history of modern Chinese intellectual thought**]
Shanghai: Sheng-huo shu-tien, 1947, Vol. 2, pp. 743-783.

The author discusses T'an in Chapter 14, entitled "Wei-hsin ssu-
hsiang te chien-che T'an Ssu-t'ung" 維新思想的健者譚嗣同 . It has four
sections, dealing respectively with the relationship between his thought
and practice, his intellectual foundation, his ideas on social reform and
his philosophical leanings. This is a fairly detailed examination of T'an's
thought, paying particular attention to the similarities and dissimilarities
between T'an and K'ang Yu-wei. The author refutes Ch'ien Mu's 錢穆
idea that T'an's martyrdom was contradictory to his radical anti-Manchu
thought and maintains that T'an sacrificed his life for the cause of
reform. The author also believes that T'an was pantheistic in his religious
thought, pro-Mohist in his philosophy of life, democratic in his political
thinking, scientific in his methodology, but he did not strictly adhere to
the historiography of the Kung-yang 公羊 School. As is evident from the
Jen-hsüeh, T'an's thought is a conglomeration of various ideas and is full
of internal contradictions.

056 **Hou Wai-lu** 侯外廬 *et al.*, ***Chung-kuo chin-tai che-hsüeh shih*** 中國近代哲
學史 [**A history of modern Chinese philosophy**]
Peking: Jen-min ch'u-pan-she, 1978, pp. 204-229.

This very recent book gives a detailed analysis of T'an's thought.
The author of the section on T'an maintains that Buddhism is the most
important school upon which the ideas in the *Jen-hsüeh* are formulated.
He examines the idealistic nature of *jen* and Ether, T'an's idealistic

epistemology, relativity, and his capitalistic ideas on human nature. The author makes many apt references to the *Hu-nan li-shih tzu-liao* 湖南歷史資料.

057 **Hou Wai-lu** 侯外廬 **(ed.),** *Wu-hsü pien-fa liu-shih chou-nien chi-nien chi* 戊戌變法六十週年紀念集 **[A commemorative volume of the sixtieth anniversary of the 1898 Reform Movement]**
Peking: Chung-hua shu-chu, 1958.

Collected here are two articles by Chang Ch'i-chih 張豈之 and Chu Jui-k'ai 祝瑞開. See respective entries.

058 **Hsiang Lin-ping** 向林冰, **"T'an Ssu-t'ung che-hsüeh te tsai p'ing-chia"** 譚嗣同哲學的再評價 **[A reappraisal of T'an Ssu-t'ung's philosophy]**
In *Li-lun yü hsien-shih* 理論與現實, Vol. 2, No. 2 (Oct. 1940), pp. 96-105.

059 **Hsiao Jen-ying** 蕭人英, **"T'an Ssu-t'ung te sheng-p'ing yü ssu-hsiang"** 譚嗣同的生平與思想 **[The life and thought of T'an Ssu-t'ung]**
Unpublished M.A. Thesis of the Institute of Historical Research, Taiwan Normal University, December 1975. 118 pages. Supervised by Professor Wang Erh-min 王爾敏.

This thesis has eight chapters. Chapter 1, Introduction, discusses the controversy over T'an's martyrdom. The author believes that T'an died in the 1898 *coup d'etat* because he was willing to shoulder the responsibility for the failure of the Hundred Days Reform, to become the forerunner of the nationalistic revolution, and to manifest the mental power of *jen*. Chapter 2 describes T'an's early life and education. Chapter 3 looks further into the changes in T'an's thought and the works he wrote. Chapter 4 assesses T'an's role in the Hunan Reform Movement. Chapter 5 examines T'an's part in the Hundred Days Reform. In Chapter 6, the author uses the term "rationalism" to describe the whole body of thought expressed in the *Jen-hsüeh*. Chapter 7 introduces the political and social thought of T'an. In his concluding chapter, the author emphasizes that apart from thought, T'an's importance in modern China also lies in his integrity and accomplishment. His heroic spirit had much to do with his belief in Buddhism and Mohism. The main thrust of the *Jen-hsüeh* is that "the *tao* pervades all things as one", and by means of it we can cast aside machinations in people's minds and strive for the creation of a synthesis of Eastern and Western cultures.

19

Writing in Taiwan, the author, regrettably, has not been able to consult some of the important works and articles published in Mainland China.

060 Hsiao Ju-lin 蕭汝霖 , "T'an Ssu-t'ung chuan" 譚嗣同傳 [A biography of T'an Ssu-t'ung]
In Min Erh-ch'ang 閔爾昌 (ed.), *Pei-chuan chi-pu* 碑傳集補 [A supplement to a collection of biographical inscriptions]. Peking: Yenching ta-hsüeh kuo-hsüeh yen-chiu-so, 1932, pp. 23-24.

An unembellished account of T'an. Not much different from Liang's biography. The author, however, is wrong in saying that T'an was the president of the Nan-hsüeh hui 南學會.

061 Hsiao Ju-lin 蕭汝霖 , *Liu-yang lieh-shih chuan* 瀏陽烈士傳 [Biographies of the martyrs of Liuyang, Hunan]
N.p., February 1913.

062 Hsiao Kung-ch'üan 蕭公權 , *Chung-kuo cheng-chih ssu-hsiang shih* 中國政治思想史 [A history of Chinese political thought]
Taipei: Chung-hua wen-hua ch'u-pan-shih-yeh wei-yüan-hui, 1954, Vol. 5, pp. 711-717.

The author says that T'an's thought was chiefly a development from K'ang Yu-wei, only that differences in character and background set them apart. T'an's ideas of having no national boundaries, of changing the traditional ethical system and eliminating the ruler-subject relationship, and of championing people's rights, were not different from K'ang's. The main difference between them, the author says, is that K'ang carried out the reform for the sake of preserving the Ch'ing dynasty, but T'an did it out of patriotism. When T'an knew that old rules could no longer work, he resorted to complete Westernization. When he knew that the Manchus would not agree to reform, he sought international intervention. But frustrated and impatient, he was moved by the exhortations of K'ang and Liang and therefore took part in the 1898 Reform Movement. The illusion he had of constitutional government, and the dependence on him of the Kuang Hsü Emperor, caused him to die for the Emperor. This, the author says, was a tragic end for such a radical thinker as T'an.

063 Hsiao Yü-ching 蕭玉井, "Kan-tan K'un-lun—wei chi-nien T'an Ssu-t'ung i-pai-i-shih nien ming-tan chi Wu-hsü liu chün-tzu hsün-nan ch'i-shih-ch'i chou-nien erh tso" 肝胆崑崙—— 爲紀念譚嗣同一百一十年冥誕及戊戌六君子殉難七十七週年而作 [Courageous were the K'un-lun friends— an essay written to commemorate the one-hundred-and-tenth birthday of the late T'an Ssu-t'ung and the seventy-seventh anniversary of the six gentlemen who died in the 1898 Reform Movement]
    In *Chuan-chi wen-hsüeh* 傳記文學, Vol. 27, No. 6 (Dec. 1975), pp. 83-85.

    A brief discussion of the allusions in T'an's last poem, with a short account of T'an's life.

064 Hsü I-chün 徐義君, "T'an Ssu-t'ung i-t'ai shuo te wei-hsin chu-i hsing-chih" 譚嗣同以太說的唯心主義性質 [On the idealistic nature of T'an Ssu-t'ung's theory of Ether]
    In *Kuang-ming jih-pao* 光明日報, 2nd February, 1962.

    In examining T'an's definitions, philosophical proclivity and thought structure, the author holds that Ether belongs to the spiritual realm. This can be ascribed to T'an's fervent interest in Buddhism and his class background.
    Criticized by Chang Li-wen.

065 Hsü Kuang-jen 徐光仁, "Chung-kuo chin-tai min-chu chu-i ch'i-meng ssu-hsiang hsien-ch'ü che—T'an Ssu-t'ung" 中國近代民主主義啓蒙思想先驅者——譚嗣同 [A pioneer of democratic and enlightenment thinking in modern China—T'an Ssu-t'ung]
    In *Chung-hsüeh li-shih chiao-hsüeh* 中學歷史教學, Vol. 9 (Sept. 1958), pp. 12-14.

    Discusses T'an's radical thought.

066 Hu Pin 胡濱, *Chung-kuo chin-tai kai-liang chu-i ssu-hsiang* 中國近代改良主義思想 [Reformist thought in modern China]
    Peking: San-lien shu-tien, 1964, pp. 140-154.

    The author describes T'an as the most radical activist in the capitalistic reformist movement of the late nineteenth century and also the most brilliant philosopher of this period. If not for his policy of compromise and his misconceptions about the Western powers, T'an would have become a democratic revolutionary. The ideas in the *Jen-hsüeh* are introduced here, with, however, no mention of the development of T'an's thought before 1896.

067 **Hu Pin** 胡濱, *Wu-hsü pien-fa* 戊戌變法 [**The 1898 Reform Movement**]
Shanghai: Hsin chih-shih ch'u-pan-she, 1956.

Pp. 48-59 deal with T'an. It is a chronological and systematic introduction to the activities and thought of the martyr. The author believes that T'an was a materialistic and progressive reformer. See also pp. 81, 95-102 on T'an's political activities in the last days of the 1898 Reform.

068 **Hu Ssu-yung** 胡思庸, **"Kao-chung k'e-pen Chung-kuo chin-tai-shih chiu-shih-san yeh: 'T'an Ssu-t'ung te Jen-hsüeh ta-sheng chi-hu ti chu-chang ch'ung-chüeh feng-chien wang-lo, tai-yu wei-wu chu-i te ch'ing-hsiang' ying-kai tsen-yang chieh-shih?"** 高中課本《中國近代史》九十三頁："譚嗣同的《仁學》大聲疾呼地主張衝決封建網羅，帶有唯物主義的傾向" 應該怎樣解釋？ [**How to explain the statement on p. 93 of *Modern Chinese History*, a textbook for senior secondary schools, which says that "T'an Ssu-t'ung was inclined to materialism as he vehemently advocated in the *Jen-hsüeh* the bursting out of all feudal enmeshing nets?"**]
In *Hsin shih-hsüeh t'ung-hsün* 新史學通訊, Vol. 7 (1955), p. 28.

The author explains that the ideas expressed in the *Jen-hsüeh* show that T'an was not confined by a feudalistic frame of thinking, and that his theory of the composition of particles was suggestive of his materialistic leanings.

069 **Hu Yüan-chün** 胡遠濬, **"T'an Ssu-t'ung Jen-hsüeh chih p'i-p'ing"** 譚嗣同 仁學之批評 [**Criticisms of T'an Ssu-t'ung's *Jen-hsüeh***]
In *Chung-yang ta-hsüeh pan-yüeh k'an* 中央大學半月刊, Vol. 2, No. 1 (Oct. 1930), pp. 109-119.

The author makes random criticisms of some ideas in the *Jen-hsüeh*, stating where they come from and how they were arbitrarily construed in the treatise. The author thinks that although T'an employed his knowledge of Western science to draw analogies with Confucian and Buddhist ideas, his understanding of these two Chinese schools of thought was in fact inadequate. Ideas examined by the author include "name and doctrine", "relativity", "sex", "frugality" and "ignorance" in Buddhism.

070 Huang Chang-chien 黃彰健, "Lun chin ch'uan T'an Ssu-t'ung yü-chung
t'i-pi shih tseng-ching Liang Ch'i-ch'ao kai-i" 論今傳譚嗣同獄中題壁詩曾
經梁啟超改易 [On the extant poem on the prison wall attributed to
T'an Ssu-t'ung being a forgery by Liang Ch'i-ch'ao]
   In Huang Chang-chien, *Wu-hsü pien-fa shih yen-chiu* 戊戌變法史研究
   [Studies on the Reform Movement of 1898]. Taipei: Chung-yang
   yen-chiu-yüan li-shih yü-yen yen-chiu-so, 1970, pp. 534-538.

   The author poses a serious challenge to the authenticity of the poem
   recorded in Liang's biography. He attempts to establish that T'an did not
   at any time inform anybody of the verse he wrote. He next suggests that
   Liang deliberately tampered with T'an's poem in order to use it for the
   purpose of saving the Emperor. Finally, he argues that another version
   of the poem which appeared in *ch'üan* 4, p. 12 of *Hsiu-hsiang K'ang
   Liang yen-i* 繡像康梁演義 is nearer to truth. This version is as follows:

   望門投止憐張儉，直諫陳書愧杜根；

   手擲歐刀仰天笑，留將公罪後人論。

   Challenged by Lo Lung-chih 羅龍治. See also the reply by the author
   in *Chung-yang jih-pao* 中央日報.

071 Huang Chang-chien 黃彰健, "T'an Ssu-t'ung ch'üan-chi shu-cha hsi-nien"
譚嗣同全集書札繫年 [Dating T'an's letters in the *Complete Works of
T'an Ssu-t'ung*]
   In *Wu-hsü pien-fa shih yen-chiu* 戊戌變法史研究, pp. 627-660.

   This is a detailed dating of all letters in *T'an Ssu-t'ung ch'üan-chi.*
   Appended with dating of letters in Ou-yang Yü-ch'ien's 歐陽予倩 *T'an
   Ssu-t'ung shu-chien* 譚嗣同書簡 and *Hu-nan li-shih tzu-liao* 湖南歷史資
   料. An indispensable reference for the study of T'an Ssu-t'ung.

072 Huang Chang-chien 黃彰健, "T'an Ssu-t'ung te yü-chung shih" 譚嗣同的
獄中詩 [T'an Ssu-t'ung's prison poem]
   In *Chung-yang jih-pao* 中央日報, 7th December, 1971.

   A reply to the doubts raised by Lo Lung-chih that *Hsiu-hsiang
   K'ang Liang yen-i* is but a popular novel, the reliability of which is
   subject to question and that the poem quoted there is therefore of
   dubious nature. The author maintains that the use of the term "*kung-
   tsui*" 公罪 (public crime) by T'an is indisputable and this explains why
   Liang needed to forge the poem. He also believes that the novel is a
   reliable source to use.

073 **Huang Te-shih** 黃得時 , **"T'an Ssu-t'ung yü T'ai-wan"** 譚嗣同與台灣.
   [T'an Ssu-t'ung and Taiwan]
   In *Chuan-chi wen-hsüeh* 傳記文學 , Vol. 10, No. 5 (May 1967),
   pp. 72-75.

   The author examines whether T'an actually did go to Taiwan as
   Liang Ch'i-ch'ao remarked, both in his biography of T'an and in the two
   poems composed in March 1911 during a fortnight's visit to Taiwan.
   The author, however, cannot find any material that would support
   Liang's view. Secondly, with the help of a friend in Tokyo, the author
   was able to obtain the original version of the *Jen-hsüeh* published in
   Japan, which did not bear the words " 台灣人所著書 " but instead had
   " 瀏陽譚壯飛先生著 ".

074 **Huang Kung-wei** 黃公偉 , **"Chin-tai ke-ming hui-hsing T'an Ssu-t'ung te
   min-chu ssu-hsiang"** 近代革命彗星譚嗣同的民主思想 **[The democratic
   thought of T'an Ssu-t'ung, a meteor of modern reformism]**
   In *Hu-nan wen-hsien* 湖南文獻 , Vol. 8 (June 1973), pp. 261-264.

   Begins with a brief biographical sketch drawn mainly from Liang's
   biography. Maintains that the idea of *jen* was developed from K'ang
   Yu-wei's thought. T'an's attack on traditional values was fierce and his
   thought was revolutionary.

075 **Huang Kung-wei** 黃公偉 , *Chung-kuo chin-tai hsüeh-shu ssu-hsiang pien-
   ch'ien shih* 中國近代學術思想變遷史 **[A history of changes in the intel-
   lectual thought in modern China]**
   Taipei: Yu-shih wen-hua shih-yeh kung-ssu, 1976, pp. 57-67.

   Identical to the above entry.

076 **Huang Kung-wei** 黃公偉 , **"T'an Ssu-t'ung yü min-chu ke-ming ssu-
   ch'ao"** 譚嗣同與民主革命思潮 **[T'an Ssu-t'ung and democratic and
   revolutionary thought]**
   In *Hsin shih-tai* 新時代 , Vol. 13, No. 6 (June 1973), pp. 18-20.

   Almost identical to the last but one entry.

077 *Hu-nan li-shih tzu-liao* 湖南歷史資料 **[Historical materials on Hunan]** ,
   Vol. 3 (1958) to Vol. 9 (1960).

   See separate entries under "T'an Ssu-t'ung".

078 Jen Chi-yü 任繼愈 *et al., Chung-kuo che-hsüeh shih chien-pien*中國哲
學史簡編 [A concise history of Chinese philosophy]
Peking: Jen-min ch'u-pan-she, 1973, pp. 551-564.

The author says that Ether is *ch'i* 氣 and that T'an's thought contains
both materialistic and spiritual elements. He also discusses the internal
contradictions in T'an's philosophy.

079 **Kao Yüeh-tien** 高越天 , **"T'an Ssu-t'ung kan-huai shih shih-chu pu-i"**
譚嗣同感懷詩釋註補疑 [Further doubtful points not dealt with in an
annotation of T'an Ssu-t'ung's poem of recollection]
In *Hsing-shih* 醒獅 , Vol. 6, No. 11 (Nov. 1968), p. 23.

080 **Kiang Shao-yuen, "The Philosophy of Tang Szu-tung"**
In *The Open Court*, Vol. 36 (1922), pp. 449-471.

This article analyses the contents of the *Jen-hsüeh* from nine angles.

081 **Ku Ch'ü** 顧曲 , **"I-p'ien shang wei shou ju T'an Ssu-t'ung chi te wen-
tzu"** 一篇尚未收入譚嗣同集的文字 [A piece of writing that is not
included in the *Complete Works of T'an Ssu-t'ung*]
In *Ch'un-chiu* 春秋 , Vol. 16, No. 4 (April 1972), pp. 41-42.

A reprint of "Wen Hsin-kuo kung Chiao-yü ch'in chi chen-chi"
文信國公蕉雨琴記真蹟 edited by Chou K'ang-hsieh 周康燮. See separate
entry under "T'an Ssu-t'ung".

082 **Kuan Huai-ch'eng** 官懷成, **"Lun T'an Ssu-t'ung che-hsüeh te chi-pen
hsing chih—chien yü Chang Li-wen t'ung-chih shang-ch'üeh"** 論譚嗣
同哲學的基本性質—— 兼與張立文同志商榷 [On the fundamental
nature of the philosophy of T'an Ssu-t'ung—a discussion with Com-
rade Chang Li-wen]
In *Kiang-han hsüeh-pao* 江漢學報, Vol. 10 (Oct. 1964), pp. 52-60.

The author asserts that T'an was basically a materialist. The reasons
being (1) *Jen* in the treatise is not of the highest category; (2) Ether is a
term generally employed in physics; (3) the brain nerves—by which
cognition is made possible—are material; and (4) Ether is a concept
partly originated from the ideas held by materialistic thinkers such as
Chang Tsai and Wang Fu-chih. But the author also concedes that T'an's
thought had an idealistic admixture.

25

083 **Kuo Chan-po** 郭湛波, *Chin-tai Chung-kuo ssu-hsiang shih* 近代中國思想
史 [A history of modern Chinese thought]
Hong Kong: Lung-men shu-tien, 1973, pp. 72-83.

Though changes have been made in other parts of this book, in this
1973 edition, the part on T'an Ssu-t'ung remains unchanged from the
1936 edition.

084 **Kuo Chan-po** 郭湛波, *Chin wu-shih nien Chung-kuo ssu-hsiang shih*
近五十年中國思想史 [A history of Chinese thought in the last fifty
years]
Reprinted in Hong Kong: Lung-men shu-tien, 1965, pp. 17-35.

This book was originally published in 1935, revised in 1936 and
reproduced in fascimile in Hong Kong in 1965. The author adopts
dialectical materialism as his viewpoint and methodology in writing
this book. He gives a brief biographical account of T'an and proceeds
to an analysis of the thought expressed in the *Jen-hsüeh*. The author
discusses the ontology, cosmology and epistemology of T'an and he
believes that T'an's political thinking stemmed mainly from K'ang Yu-wei.

085 **Kwong, Luke S. K.** 鄺兆江, "Reflections on an Aspect of Modern China
in Transition: T'an Ssu-t'ung (1865-1898) as a Reformer"
In Paul A. Cohen and John E. Schrecker (ed.), *Reform in Nineteenth-
Century China*. Cambridge, Mass: East Asian Research Centre,
Harvard University, 1976, pp. 184-193.

The author first examines why T'an gradually became a psychologi-
cally complex person and finds that it was the crisis both from within
and without, aggravated by China's defeat in the Sino-Japanese War,
which resulted in his own awakening, symbolized by his intention to
"fly high". But T'an as a reform-minded literatus had his ambivalence.
His dilemmas were (1) actual adhesion to a behavioural pattern vis-a-vis
the quest for liberation; (2) an intention to better society but also a
feeling of detachment from the indigenous establishment; and (3) the
hope of building an ideal society but insufficient experiences in
mundane affairs. The author also suggests that in T'an there were
reflected the rising expectations of a transitional generation of literati
and that the "failure" of T'an's efforts showed "a dreary scarcity of
resources in late Ch'ing society for coping with the challenge of a highly
protean and dynamic transitional generation."

086 Lan Chi-fu 藍吉富, "T'an Ssu-t'ung yü fo-hsüeh" 譚嗣同與佛學 [T'an Ssu-t'ung and Buddhism]

In *Hsin-hsia* 新夏, Vol. 27 (March 1972), pp. 14-15.

The author explains that T'an's ardent interest in Buddhism is manifested in his elimination of the differences between the self and others, his enthusiasm for national salvation and his spirited courage.

087 Li Ao 李敖, "Liang K'un-lun k'ao" 兩崑崙考 [Examining the allusions of "liang K'un-lun"]

In *Li-shih yü jen-hsiang* 歷史與人像 [History and portraits]. Taipei: Wen-hsing shu-tien, 1964, pp. 77-81.

Examines who were the two persons T'an alluded to.

088 Li Hung-ch'iu 李鴻球, "T'an Ssu-t'ung T'ang Ts'ai-ch'ang liang hsien-lieh pai-nien chi-nien" 譚嗣同唐才常兩先烈百年紀念 [The centennial anniversary of the two martyrs T'an Ssu-t'ung and T'ang Ts'ai-ch'ang]

In *Tzu-li wan-pao* 自立晚報, 4th December, 1966, p. 4.

089 Li Shao-ling 李少陵, "T'an Ssu-t'ung ts'ung-jung chiu-i" 譚嗣同從容就義 [T'an Ssu-t'ung met martyrdom with perfect composure]

In *Kung-pao yüeh-k'an* 公報月刊, Vol. 2, No. 4 (Dec. 1969), p. 11.

090 Li Tse-hou 李澤厚, *K'ang Yu-wei T'an Ssu-t'ung ssu-hsiang yen-chiu* 康有爲譚嗣同思想研究 [Studies on the thought of K'ang Yu-wei and T'an Ssu-t'ung]

Shanghai: Jen-min ch'u-pan-she, 1958, pp. 159-235.

Contains revised versions of the following two articles.

091 Li Tse-hou 李澤厚, "Kuan-yü T'an Ssu-t'ung che-hsüeh ssu-hsiang te yen-chiu—tui Sun Ch'ang-chiang hsien-sheng liang-p'ien wen-chang te i-hsieh i-chien" 關於譚嗣同哲學思想的研究—— 對孫長江先生兩篇文章的一些意見 [On the study of T'an Ssu-t'ung's philosophical thought —some comments on the two articles by Mr. Sun Ch'ang-chiang]

In *Che-hsüeh yen-chiu* 哲學研究, Vol. 3 (June 1957), pp. 68-86.

Also included in Chou K'ang-hsieh 周康燮 (ed.), *Chung-kuo chin san-pai-nien hsüeh-shu ssu-hsiang lun-chi ssu-pien* 中國近三百年學術思想論集四編 [Fourth collection of articles on Chinese learning and thought of the last three hundred years]. Hong Kong: Ch'ung-wen shu-tien, 1973, pp. 150-168.

Collected in the author's *K'ang yu-wei T'an Ssu-t'ung ssu-hsiang yen-chiu,* pp. 208-235.

A reply to Sun Ch'ang-chiang's criticisms. Still maintaining that Ether is defined by T'an as a molecular substance, the author further points out that Sun's view that Ether is *jen* and that the difference between the two lies only in their "name and origin" is unfounded. Ether and *jen*, the author bluntly states, are two concepts which cannot be equated. The relationship between them is precisely the same as that between *ch'i* and *tao*. Ether may be described as a kind of supremely subtle metaphysical substance with an abstract nature. In this sense, Ether and *jen* are the same. This similarity also causes the concept of Ether to acquire a pantheistic character. Sun Ch'ang-chiang, the author points out, has failed to see the Ether-*jen* relationship in the light of a *ch'i-tao* one. He has thus ignored the sharp internal contradiction in the whole of T'an's philosophy. As to the relationship between Ether and mental power, the author also believes that they are not interchangeable. Ether is materialistic. Moreover, the text of the *Jen-hsüeh* and his article "I-t'ai shuo" 以太說 [On Ether] clearly show that Ether is far more fundamental than mental power.

092 **Li Tse-hou** 李澤厚, **"Lun T'an Ssu-t'ung te che-hsüeh ssu-hsiang ho she-hui cheng-chih kuan-tien"** 論譚嗣同的哲學思想和社會政治觀點 **[On T'an Ssu-t'ung's philosophical thought and social and political views]**
In *Hsin chien-she* 新建設, Vol. 7 (July 1955), pp. 49-62.
    Also included in Chou K'ang-hsieh 周康燮 (ed.), *Chung-kuo chin san-pai-nien hsüeh-shu ssu-hsiang lun-chi erh-pien* 中國近三百年學術思想論集二編 [Second collection of articles on Chinese learning and thought of the last three hundred years]. Hong Kong: Ch'ung-wen shu-tien, 1971, pp. 209-223.
    Included in Chou K'ang-hsieh 周康燮 (ed.), *Chung-kuo chin san-pai-nien hsüeh-shu ssu-hsiang lun-chi ssu-pien* 中國近三百年學術思想論集四編 [Fourth collection of articles on Chinese learning and thought of the last three hundred years]. Hong Kong: Ch'ung-wen shu-tien, 1973, pp. 135-149.
    Collected in the author's *K'ang Yu-wei T'an Ssu-t'ung ssu-hsiang yen-chiu*, pp. 150-168.

The author wrote this article to commemorate the ninetieth anniversary of T'an's birth. He believes that T'an's thought, characterized by his patriotism, was shaped by his class standing, his time, his interest in Buddhism, his willingness to synthesize different schools of thought and his intention to follow K'ang Yu-wei. In explaining the interrelatedness of the four major concepts—*jen*, Ether, mental power and t'ung 通, the author says that *jen* in T'an's thought is the law of the universe, the content of which is *t'ung*. *T'ung* can be understood as the unity of things. Therefore, the *"jen-t'ung"* relationship has two aspects: its dialectic aspect—which includes the notions of "identification", "daily renovation" and "relativity"; and its sophistical aspect—which is demonstrated by his ideas on the relationship between name and doctrine. As to the *"jen*-Ether" relationship, the author thinks that it has to be understood in two ways. First, Ether is the material foundation of *jen*, which means Ether is the substance of *jen* while *jen* is the function of Ether. The origin of such a line of reasoning can be traced to T'an's earlier subscription to the *tao-ch'i* concept. Second, because of T'an's inadequate knowledge of the original notion of Ether, he gives it a metaphysical coating, and thus a pantheistic character. In this way, *jen* and Ether are one. T'an's socio-political viewpoints, the author maintains, were direct logical deductions from his philosophical premises. Thus, on the one hand, his materialistic *jen-t'ung* concepts gave rise to radical reformist ideas, but on the other hand, his idealistic theory of mental power also formed the foundation of his reactionary social and religious thinking.

093 **Liang Ch'i-ch'ao** 梁啟超 , ***Ch'ing-tai hsüeh-shu kai-lun*** 清代學術概論 **[An introduction to the scholarship of the Ch'ing dynasty]**
Originally published in Shanghai, 1921. Reprinted in Taipei: Chunghua shu-chü, 1971, pp. 66-69.

The author, himself a very close friend of T'an, was an authoritative interpreter of T'an's thought. Since almost all of what he had earlier written on T'an was frequently quoted in works dealing with the martyr, a more faithful rendering of his views on T'an was deemed necessary. He thinks that T'an was a meteor of the late Ch'ing intellectual world. T'an's learning underwent a change when he met the author, and yet another change when he learned Buddhism from Yang Wen-hui 楊文會 . The spirit of the *Jen-hsüeh* was akin to Issac Newton's iconoclasm. The intention behind the treatise was to mould science, philosophy and religion into one. The author then introduces the main ideas of the *Jen-hsüeh*, adding that the main thrust of his political thought was universalism.

094 **Liang Ch'i-ch'ao** 梁啟超 , *Intellectual Trends in the Ch'ing Period*
Translated by Immanuel C. Y. Hsu. Cambridge, Mass: Harvard University Press, 1959, pp. 107-110.

English translation of the above entry.

095 Liang Ch'i-ch'ao 梁啟超, "Yin-ping shih shih-hua" 飲冰室詩話 [Remarks
     on poems from the Ice-drinking Studio]
         In *Hsin-min tsung-pao* 新民叢報, Vol. 4 (24th March, 1902), pp. 1-2.

     The author thinks that T'an's poems inaugurated a new era in late
     Ch'ing poetry. Such is evident in his poems "Kan-huai" 感懷 (*T'an Ssu-
     t'ung ch'üan-chi* 譚嗣同全集 [Complete works of T'an Ssu-t'ung],
     hereafter as *TSTCC*, p. 484), and "Chü-hua yen ming—tseng Liang
     Jen-kung tso" 菊花硯銘—— 贈梁任公作 (*TSTCC*, p. 501).

096 Liang Ch'i-ch'ao 梁啟超, "T'an Ssu-t'ung chuan" 譚嗣同傳 [A bio-
     graphy of T'an Ssu-t'ung]
         In *Ch'ing-i pao* 清議報, Vol. 4 (22nd January, 1899), pp. 4-7. Repro-
     duced in fascimile in Taipei: Cheng-wen ch'u-pan-she, 1967.

     The most quoted biography. Brief and lucid, but sometimes not too
     reliable. It concludes with a very Buddhistic interpretation of T'an's
     learning.

097 Liang Ch'i-ch'ao 梁啟超, "T'an lieh-fu chuan" 譚烈婦傳 [A sketch of
     the virtuous Mrs. T'an Ssu-t'ung]
         In *Ch'ing-i pao* 清議報, Vol. 10 (1st April, 1899), pp. 4a-4b.

     Reprinted from *T'ientsin kuo-wen pao* 天津國聞報. It describes Mrs.
     T'an as a virtuous woman devoted to her husband. When she learned
     of his death, she several times attempted suicide, first by jumping into a
     river when taking a ferry, then by banging her head against the floor
     in Ch'en Pao-chien's 陳寶箴 residence. But she did not die. The following
     day, however, she again hit her head against the bed and died as a result
     of serious wounds. The blood which poured over her chest formed the
     character *tao* 刀 (knife).
         See T'an Hsün-ts'ung 譚訓聰 for the untenability of this account.
     Also the account by Lin Kuang-hao 林光灝.

098 Lin I-hsin 林一新, "T'an Ssu-t'ung te ssu-hsiang chi ch'i yü ju-fo chih
     kuan-hsi" 譚嗣同的思想及其與儒佛之關係 [The thought of T'an Ssu-
     t'ung and its relationship to Confucianism and Buddhism]
         In *Wen-hua chien-she* 文化建設, Vol. 1, No. 12 (Sept. 1935),
     pp. 39-48.

     A rather substantial article dealing with the relationship of the
     three major religious schools in the *Jen-hsüeh*. The author emphatically

points out that the Buddhist methodology was T'an's major tool for explaining the world. Like Liang Ch'i-ch'ao, the author regards T'an as "the most advanced religious reformer with progressive thinking" during modern China's renaissance.

099 **Lin Jui-ming** 林瑞明 **, "T'an Ssu-t'ung pien-t'ung kuan te hsing-ch'eng yü shih-chien"** 譚嗣同變通觀的形成與實踐 **[The formation and practice of T'an Ssu-t'ung's idea of change]**
In *Shih-yüan* 史原 , Vol. 7 (Oct. 1976), pp. 115-144.

An article inspired partly by Lin Tsai-chüeh's 林載爵 M.A. thesis. It traces the stages of intellectual development of T'an and examines the content of the *Jen-hsüeh*.

100 **Lin Kuang-hao** 林光灝 **, "T'an Ssu-t'ung fu-jen te hsün-chieh ku-shih"** 譚嗣同夫人的殉節故事 **[The virtuous story of Mrs. T'an Ssu-t'ung]**
In *I wen chih* 藝文誌 , Vol. 27 (Dec. 1967), p. 13.

An account of Mrs. T'an Ssu-t'ung as a virtuous woman. It intends to refute Tso Shun-sheng's 左舜生 idea that T'an's marriage was not a happy one. The article closely follows Liang's account.
Criticized by T'an Hsün-ts'ung 譚訓聰 .

101 **Lin Tsai-chüeh** 林載爵 **,** *T'an Ssu-t'ung* 譚嗣同 **[T'an Ssu-t'ung]**
Vol. 48 of Wang Shou-nan 王壽南 (ed.), *Chung-kuo li-tai ssu-hsiang chia* 中國歷代思想家 [Chinese thinkers down the ages]. Taipei: Shang-wu yin-shu-kuan, 1978. 86 pages (pp. 5517-5608).

A condensed version of his M.A. thesis without footnotes. No apparent changes in his basic approach and in his conclusions.

102 **Lin Tsai-chüeh** 林載爵 **, "T'an Ssu-t'ung p'ing-chuan"** 譚嗣同評傳 **[An interpretative biography of T'an Ssu-t'ung]**
M.A. thesis of the Institute of Historical Research, Tung Hai University, Taiwan, 1975. 312 pages. Supervised by Professor Lü Shih-p'eng 呂士朋 .

This thesis has seven chapters. Chapter 1 describes T'an's youth and his romantic character. Chapter 2 explains how, under the impact of external factors, T'an awoke to the disastrous situation facing China. In 1885, his "Chih yen" 治言 revealed his ethnocentric views. In 1893, his "Shih-chü ying lu pi-chih" 石菊影廬筆識 showed a change in his parochialism; he began to see the importance of assimilating Western learning into traditional Chinese culture. In 1894, shocked by China's defeat in the Sino-Japanese War, T'an had an awakening and opted for reform. Chapter 3 describes T'an's activities in Hupeh, Hunan, Nanking and Hunan again during 1895-1898. Chapter 4 accounts for T'an's ambivalent feelings toward reform and describes his last tragic days. Chapter 5 gives a very substantial analysis of the philosophical, social, political and economic thought of the *Jen-hsüeh*. Chapter 6 puts T'an in the intellectual trends of late Ch'ing. In explaining the conceptual transition from *yang-wu* 洋務 to *tao-ch'i* 道器 and to *pien-fa* 變法 , the author points out that T'an's assertation that *tao* has universality is the final stage of the *tao-ch'i* development. In the *pien-fa* stage, syncretism is the main theme, which is also evident in the *Jen-hsüeh*. To syncretize without adequate knowledge easily commits two mistakes: formalism and pan-scientism. The chapter ends with a discussion of how T'an's *Jen-hsüeh* reflected the harmonization of the trends of tradition and anti-tradition. Chapter 7 concludes with an examination of T'an's historical vision. His case reflected the conscious change of a late Ch'ing intellectual from a traditional mind to one equipped with technical knowledge. T'an was a utopian. When he tried to put his ideas into practice, he was helpless against corrupt officialdom. Finally, his martyrdom paved the way for the Revolution of 1911; his *Jen-hsüeh* represented a final vain effort in the late 1890s to defend the traditional Chinese cultural order.

103 **Lin Tsai-chüeh** 林載爵 , **"T'an Ssu-t'ung yü wan-Ch'ing ssu-hsiang te ch'ü-shih"** 譚嗣同與晚清思想的趨勢 [**T'an Ssu-t'ung and intellectual trends in the late Ch'ing**]
   In *Shih-hsüeh hui-k'an* 史學會刊, Vol. 3 (June 1975), pp. 26-37.

   Same as Chapter 6 of the last entry.

104 **Liu Chi-ta** 劉己達 , **"T'an Ssu-t'ung yü Ta-tao Wang Wu"** 譚嗣同與大刀王五 [**T'an Ssu-t'ung and Great Sword Wang Wu**]
   In *Chung-wai tsa-chih* 中外雜誌, Vol. 5, No. 3 (1969), pp. 10-12.

   A relatively detailed description of Ta-tao Wang Wu's life and his anecdotes. Interesting and informative.

105 **Lo Chu-feng** 羅竹風 , **"Tu Liang Ch'i-chao T'an Ssu-t'ung chuan so hsiang-tao te"** 讀梁啟超譚嗣同傳所想到的 [**Thoughts aroused by reading**

Liang Ch'i-ch'ao's "Biography of T'an Ssu-t'ung"]
  In *Yü-wen chiao-hsüeh* 語文教學, Vol. 12 (Dec. 1957), pp. 1-3.

Describes Liang's literary skill in his presentation of facts in the biography.

106 **Lo Lung-chih** 羅龍治, **"Wang Wu yü T'an Ssu-t'ung"** 王五與譚嗣同
    [Wang Wu and T'an Ssu-t'ung]
    In *Chung-yang jih-pao* 中央日報, 1st December, 1971.

A description of Wang Wu and an examination of the various interpretations of the term "Liang K'un-lun" 兩崑崙 in T'an's last poem. The author is of the opinion that 'K'un-lun nu' 崑崙奴 may allude to the swordsman mentioned in the *ch'uan-ch'i* 傳奇 by P'ei Hsing 裴鉶 of the T'ang dynasty. He also doubts Huang Chang-chien's 黃彰健 proposition that the poem was tampered with by Liang Ch'i-ch'ao and that the one recorded in *Hsiu-hsiang K'ang Liang yen-i* 繡像康梁演義 should be adopted.
  See the reply by Huang Chang-chien.

107 **Lu T'ang-p'ing** 魯蕩平, **"T'an Ssu-t'ung pei sha nei-mu chi Ch'ing Te-tsung shang-yü"** 譚嗣同被殺內幕及清德宗上諭 **[The inside story of the execution of T'an Ssu-t'ung and the imperial edict of the Kuang-hsü Emperor]**
    In *Hu-nan wen-hsien* 湖南文獻, Vol. 5 (Aug. 1971), pp. 62-63.

Argues that it was Kuang-hsü who demanded the execution of T'an without trial, because he feared that he might get involved in the whole incident. This is borne out by the imperial edict of the Emperor.

108 **Lü Wei-tung** 呂偉東, **"T'an Ssu-t'ung kan-huai shih shih-chu"** 譚嗣同感懷詩釋註 **[An annotation of T'an Ssu-t'ung's poem of recollection]**
    In *Hsing-shih* 醒獅, Vol. 6, No. 9 (Sept. 1968), pp. 20-21.

109 **Nan Hu** 南湖 **[Kao Pai-shih** 高拜石**]**, **"P'i Lu-men shih tao T'an Ssu-t'ung"** 皮鹿門詩悼譚嗣同 **[Pi Hsi-jui mourning T'an Ssu-t'ung with a poem]**
    In *Chung-yang jih-pao* 中央日報, 27th March, 1962.

A brief description of Pi Hsi-jui 皮錫瑞 with a few remarks on the circumstances under which the poem was written.

110 **Nan Hu** 南湖, **"T'an Ssu-t'ung i-shih yü i-tso"** 譚嗣同佚事與佚作
[Hitherto unknown anecdotes and writings of T'an Ssu-t'ung]
In *Chung-yang jih-pao* 中央日報, 2nd September, 1961.

111 **Nan Hu** 南湖, **"T'an Ssu-t'ung shih-wen chün-yung"** 譚嗣同詩文雋永
[Outstanding and long-lasting are the poems and essays of T'an Ssu-t'ung]
In *Chung-yang jih-pao* 中央日報, 18th November, 1961.

112 **Oka, Takashi, "The Philosophy of T'an Ssu-t'ung"**
In *Papers on China*, Vol. 9 (Aug. 1955), pp. 1-47.

Introduces the philosophical thought of T'an and concludes that T'an was a faithful Confucian. Following the views of Fung Yu-lan, the author regards T'an as one of the last Chinese thinkers who belonged to the "period of classical learning".

113 **Onogawa, Hidemi** 小野川秀美, **"T'an Ssu-t'ung te pien-ke lun—chi ch'i hsing-ch'eng kuo-ch'eng"** 譚嗣同的變革論一及其形成過程 **[T'an Ssu-t'ung's reformist thought, and its process of formation]**
Translated by Li Yung-ch'ih 李永熾, *Ta-lu tsa-chih* 大陸雜誌, Vol. 38, No. 10 (May 1969), pp. 23-32.

Uses the letters of T'an as a basis for exploring the development of T'an's reformist thought. A very substantial article originally written in Japanese.

114 **Ou-yang Pan-chiang** 歐陽瓣薑 **[Ou-yang Chung-ku** 歐陽中鵠**]** *et al.*, **"Pan-chiang wen-kuo ho Wei-lu jih-chi chung kuan-yü Liu-yang hsing-hsüeh te tzu-liao"** 瓣薑文稿和蔚廬日記中關於瀏陽興學的資料 **[Materials in the draft writings of Ou-yang Chung-ku and the diary of Liu Jen-hsi concerning the promotion of the learning of mathematics in Liu-yang]**
In Hu-nan sheng-chih hsüeh-shu-chih pien-chi hsiao-tsu 湖南省志學術志編輯小組 (ed.), *Hu-nan li-shih tzu-liao* 湖南歷史資料, Vol. 7 (Sept. 1959), pp. 135-155.

Contains excerpts of diaries from Liu Jen-hsi 劉人熙 and letters of Ou-yang Chung-ku relating to T'an's ideas of promoting the learning of mathematics in Liuyang, Hunan.

115 Ou-yang Yü-ch'ien 歐陽予倩 (ed.), *T'an Ssu-t'ung shu-chien* 譚嗣同書簡 [The letters of T'an Ssu-t'ung]
    Shanghai: Wen-hua kung-ying she, 1948. 138 pages.

Included here are a preface by the author (which was originally published as "T'an Ssu-t'ung shu-chien hsu" 譚嗣同書簡序 [Preface to the *Letters of T'an Ssu-t'ung*] in *Wen-hua tsa-chih* 文化雜誌 , Vol. 2. No. 1 (April 1942), pp. 53–54), a collection of twenty-seven letters from T'an to Ou-yang Chung-ku. Appended to these are nine letters from T'ang Ts'ai-ch'ang 唐才常 to Ou-yang Chung-ku and fourteen letters from the latter to T'an. All these letters are undated. See Huang Chang-chien for their dating.

116 P'ang Pu 龐 朴 , "Lüeh-lun T'an Ssu-t'ung te che-hsüeh ssu-hsiang" 略論 譚嗣同的哲學思想 [A brief discussion of T'an Ssu-t'ung's philosophical ideas]
    In *Hsin chien-she* 新建設 , Vol. 6 (June 1962), pp. 48–54.

The author summarizes the different views of the nature of T'an's thinking and emphasizes that T'an's thought is immature and full of internal contradictions. Taking apparently no particular stance, the author says that there are both materialistic and idealistic elements in T'an's thought. When he uses the general and objective nature of Ether to explain the phenomenal world, he is materialistic. When, in order to explain spiritual phenomena, he maintains that Ether has consciousness, he goes into vulgar hylozoism; with his belief in the immortality of the soul, he becomes an idealist; and when he uses mental power to explain social phenomena, he is a historical idealist. In conclusion, the author says that there are fundamental contradictions in T'an's philosophy, which is in need of detailed analysis. This being so, the complicated philosophical conglomeration in the *Jen-hsüeh* should not be simply labelled as either idealistic or materialistic.
    Criticized by Chang Li-wen 張立文.

117 Robel, R. Ronald, "The Life and Thought of T'an Ssu-t'ung"
    Unpublished Ph.D. thesis of the University of Michigan, 1972. 458 pages.

This thesis, including Introduction, has seven chapters. Chapter 1 deals with T'an's early life and is divided into two sections—before and after 1875. The first section concentrates on T'an's life in Peking and

35

the various events which characterized his childhood. The second deals with his travels to Hunan and Kansu and attempts to describe the kinds of experience which affected his life. The concluding portion of this chapter is devoted to an examination of the "Chih yen" 治言 essay.

Chapter 2 describes the cultural tradition and historical events which played a part in T'an's attitudes. Chapter 3 analyses the crucial years from 1889 to 1895 when T'an became fascinated by Western learning and began to revise many of his previous opinions. It was during this period that T'an became convinced of the need for reform and made his first modest efforts in that direction. The last portion of the chapter contains a discussion of T'an's numerous writings from these years.

Chapter 4 covers the *Jen-hsüeh* 仁學 period. The first part deals with his personal life and activities and the last contains a description of the *Jen-hsüeh*, along with an analysis of certain aspects of this treatise.

The fifth chapter deals with the Hunan Reform programme and T'an's participation in this interesting experiment. Included in this account is a description of some of T'an's speeches and essays composed while he was staying in Ch'angsha. The concluding chapter describes the final weeks of T'an's life and his role in the national reform programme of 1898.

118 **Robel, R. Ronald, "T'an Ssu-t'ung on Hsüeh Hui 學會 or Study Association"**

In Frederic Evans Wakeman (ed.), *Nothing Concealed: Essays in Honor of Liu Yu-yün*. Taipei: Chinese Materials and Research Aids Service Centre, 1970, pp. 161-176.

This article traces the historical background of the formation of study association in the late Ch'ing. It analyses T'an's ideas on the function of the study association. The main source for the discussion is "Chuang-fei lou chih-shih shih-p'ien" 壯飛樓治事十篇, particularly essays one, two, three and four. The last two are translated in full at the end of the article.

119 **Shek, Richard, H., "Some Western Influences on T'an Ssu-t'ung's Thought"**

In Paul A. Cohen and John E. Schrecker (ed.), *Reform in Nineteenth-Century China*. Cambridge, Mass.: East Asian Research Center, Harvard University, 1976, pp. 194-203.

Examines the influence of the West upon T'an through two publications—*Wan-kuo kung-pao* 萬國公報 and *Chih-hsin mien-ping-fa* 治心免病法. The former provided a source of radicalism to T'an, largely through the lucid expositions by its most prolific contributor, the Rev. Alexander Williamson, about spiritual equality, and personal, moral and religious autonomy. This resulted in T'an's quest for a more democratic form of government and a more egalitarian society which called into question the validity of the Confucian percept "three bonds and five relationships". The book *Chih-hsin mien-ping-fa* was closely related to T'an's formulation of the concept Ether and the idea of *t'ung* 通, his denigration of the physical body and thus his commitment to martyrdom.

120 **Shih Chun** 石峻 *et al.*, *Chung-kuo chin-tai ssu-hsiang shih chiang-shou t'i-kang* 中國近代思想史講授提綱 [**Main points for lecturing on the history of modern Chinese thought**]
Peking: Jen-min ch'u-pan-she, 1957, pp. 79-87.

A summary introduction to T'an's thought. The author holds that T'an was essentially a materialist. Some idealist negative thinking apart, T'an was a great enlightenment thinker, a democrat, and the forerunner of materialism in modern China (p. 86).

121 **Shih Chun** 石峻 *et al.* **(ed.),** *Chung-kuo chin-tai ssu-hsiang shih ts'an-k'ao tzu-liao chien-p'ien* 中國近代思想史參考資料簡編 [**Selected reference materials on modern Chinese intellectual history**]
Peking: San-lien shu-tien, 1957.

122 **Ssu-ma Wen** 司馬文, **"Ts'ung tui Tung Chung-shu T'an Ssu-t'ung che-hsüeh te mou-hsieh fen-hsi t'an ch'i"** 從對董仲舒譚嗣同哲學的某些分析談起 [**A discussion arising out of certain analyses of the philosophies of Tung Chung-shu and T'an Ssu-t'ung**]
In *Kuang-ming jih-pao* 光明日報, 4th November, 1963.

123 **Su Hsüeh-lin** 蘇雪林, **"T'an Liu-yang kan-huai ssu-lü i-ts'e"** 譚瀏陽感懷四律臆測 [**A conjectural interpretation of T'an Ssu-t'ung's poem "My feelings"**]
In *Tung-fang tsa-chih* 東方雜誌, Vol. 2, No. 2 (Aug. 1968), pp. 38-43.

124 **Sun Ch'ang-chiang** 孫長江, **"Kuan-yü T'an Ssu-t'ung che-hsüeh ssu-hsiang yen-chiu te chi-ko wen-t'i—tsai ho Li Tse-hou t'ung-chih shang-chüeh"** 關於譚嗣同哲學思想研究的幾個問題——再和李澤厚同志商榷 [**Con-**

cerning several problems in the study of the philosophical thought of
T'an Ssu-t'ung—a further discussion with Comrade Li Tse-hou]
  In *Chiao-hsüeh yü yen-chiu* 教學與研究 , Vol. 10 (Oct. 1957), pp. 63-
69.

  A reply to Li Tse-hou's 1957 article in *Che-hsüeh yen-chiu* 哲學研究.
The author examines several questions related to the study of T'an's
thought. The author thinks that Ether is not materialistic but idealistic
in nature. Ether is not an abstract materialistic concept, since the
orthodox definition of "dialectic materialism" says it is not. Mental
power, as opposed to Ether, is idealistic. As to whether T'an's philo-
sophy is subjective or objective idealism, Sun maintains that since Wei-
shih 唯識 Buddhism is the foundation of his thought, it cannot but be
subjective idealism. Li Tse-hou has said that T'an's methodology is
dialectical, his epistemology is relativist, and his ontology is "the theory
of mental power". Sun says that since the "theory of mental power" is
the basis of relativism, Li's statement that T'an's epistemology is
dominated by relativism is tautological. As to Li's idea that T'an
believes cognition has an end, he is wrong. When T'an says that "when
karma-consciousness is transformed to wisdom this is the end of con-
sciousness," he is in fact talking about relative truth and absolute truth.
T'an is an agnostic. The common metaphysical ground upon which
T'an's methodology, epistemology and ontology stand is their idealistic
nature. As to the question of the class standing of T'an's thought, the
author says that Li is inconsistent. At one time, he regards T'an as "an
intellectual of the lower social stratum", at another, "a reformer of the
noble class". In conclusion, the author maintains that, other minor
foibles apart, he is still right in regarding T'an as an idealist because of
the time and the class standing that conditioned him, and above all,
because of his fervent application of Buddhist doctrines to his political
thought.

125 Sun Ch'ang-chiang 孫長江 , "Lun T'an Ssu-t'ung" 論譚嗣同 [On T'an
Ssu-t'ung]
  In *Li-shih yen-chiu* 歷史研究 , Vol. 3 (June 1965), pp. 53-74.
    Also included in Chou K'ang-hsieh 周康燮 (ed.), *Chung-kuo chin
san-pai-nien hsüeh-shu ssu-hsiang lun-chi erh-pien* 中國近三百年學
術思想論集二編 [Second collection of articles on Chinese learning
and thought of the last three hundred years]. Hong Kong: Ch'ung-
wen shu-tien, 1971, pp. 187-208.

A very detailed examination of the thought of T'an, concentrating on its development and the major philosophical cornerstones of the *Jen-hsüeh* and his political and economic ideas. The author, as always, believes that T'an was basically an idealist.

126 Sun Ch'ang-chiang 孫長江, "Shih lun T'an Ssu-t'ung" 試論譚嗣同 [A tentative discussion of T'an Ssu-t'ung]

In *Chiao-hsüeh yü yen-chiu* 教學與研究, Vol. 10 (Oct. 1955), pp. 16-25.

Also collected in Chung-kuo jen-min ta-hsüeh Chung-kuo li-shih chiao-yen shih 中國人民大學中國歷史教研室 (ed.), *Chung-kuo chin-tai ssu-hsiang-chia yen-chiu lun-wen hsüan* 中國近代思想家研究論文選 [A selection of articles on modern Chinese thinkers]. Peking: San-lien shu-tien, 1957, pp. 34-62.

The origins of T'an's thought are multifarious, but mainly drawn from Western science, late Ming anti-feudal thought, K'ang Yu-wei and Mahayana Buddhism. Ether is the substance of the universe. His views of development——daily renovation, the denial of the self and of time, and relativism, are all effective theoretical tools for combatting conservatism. T'an's thought is subjective idealism because (1) the monistic Ether, in T'an's philosophical context, is idealistic, for it is a concept infused by Wei-shih Buddhism; (2) the function-substance relationship of Ether emphasizes consciousness. His political views are characterized by (1) democratic views that rulers are not different from subjects in status or in power; and hence his anti-Manchu attitude; (2) his pro-Western attitude, and unbounded belief in mechanization and free enterprise. But he did not see the true nature of imperialism. In conclusion, T'an is regarded here as an idealist and a representative of the fast growing capitalist class.

127 Sun Ch'ang-chiang 孫長江, "T'an Ssu-t'ung shih wei-wu chu-i che ma? P'ing Li Tse-hou t'ung-chih tui T'an Ssu-t'ung che-hsüeh ssu-hsiang te p'ing-chia" 譚嗣同是唯物主義者嗎？評李澤厚同志對譚嗣同哲學思想的評價 [Was T'an Ssu-t'ung a materialist? Comments on Comrade Li Tse-hou's appraisal of T'an Ssu-t'ung's philosophical thought]

In *Chiao-hsüeh yü yen-chiu* 教學與研究, Vol. 10 (Oct. 1956).

In response to Li Tse-hou's reply, the author points out that, contrary to Li, T'an actually did not say that the universe is made up of elements

39

but of "the element of elements", Ether. In the definition of dialectic materialism, the author maintains, Ether is not an abstract materialistic concept; it is, in the final analysis, that which governs the entire universe. According to T'an, Ether is a name borrowed to denote mental power and is mere-consciousness. This is idealistic. And since he further asserts that all phenomena are the creation of mind, T'an's thought is unquestionably subjective idealism. Other factors, like his agnostic attitude and the all-embracing role Buddhism plays in his thought, show very clearly that T'an is an idealist.

128 **Sun Ch'ang-chiang** 孫長江, **"T'an Ssu-t'ung te Jen-hsüeh"** 譚嗣同的仁學 [The *Jen-hsüeh* of T'an Ssu-t'ung]
    In *Tu-shu yüeh-pao* 讀書月報, Vol. 2 (Feb. 1958), pp. 20-21.

Briefly introduces the ideas expressed in the *Jen-hsüeh*.

129 **Sun Ch'ang-chiang** 孫長江 **and Chang Li-wen** 張立文, **"Lun T'an Ssu-t'ung"** 論譚嗣同 [On T'an Ssu-t'ung]
    In San-lien shu-tien pien-chi pu 三聯書店編輯部 (ed.), *Chung-kuo chin-tai jen-wu lun-ts'ung* 中國近代人物論叢 [A collection of essays on modern Chinese personalities]. Peking: San-lien shu-tien, 1965, pp. 157-177.

An article specially written for the book. As such, it is by and large an introduction to the life and thought of T'an, and seldom touches on the philosophical aspects of T'an's thought.

130 **Sung Che** 宋哲, **"T'an Ssu-t'ung te cheng-chih ssu-hsiang"** 譚嗣同的政治思想 [The political thought of T'an Ssu-t'ung]
    In *Cheng-chih p'ing-lun* 政治評論, Vol. 2, No. 10 (May 1958), pp. 23-24.

If T'an had not died young, the author says, he could have become a revolutionary. This can be seen from his political thought which was anti-Manchu, anti-imperialist, and skeptical of conservatism in Confucian thought. T'an pointed out that what made China a semi-feudal and semi-colonial society was autocracy, which should be replaced by the democratic form of government. People, moreover, should be given freedom to vent their opinions.

131 **Talbott, Nathan M., "Intellectual Origins and Aspects of Political**

Thought in the 'Jen-hsüeh' of T'an Ssu-t'ung, Martyr of the 1898 Reform"
Unpublished Ph.D. thesis of Washington University, 1956. 388 pages.

This thesis has three parts. Part 1 introduces and summarizes the content of the *Jen-hsüeh*. Part 2 traces the intellectual basis and origins of the treatise by examining each major influence in turn. Part 3 gives conclusions. By and large, this doctoral thesis is an early but unsuccessful attempt to examine the different intellectual schools which played a part in the thought of the *Jen-hsüeh*. Bearing in mind the availability of sources and the level of Sinology in the West at that time, the shortcomings of this thesis are understandable.

132 Talbott, Nathan M., "T'an Ssu-t'ung and the Ether"
In Robert K. Sakai (ed.), *Studies on Asia*. Lincoln, Nebraska: University of Nebraska Press, 1960, pp. 20-30.

Examines the substance and function of Ether as elucidated in the *Jen-hsüeh*. The author then discusses briefly the evolution of the concept of Ether in the West to show that T'an's understanding of it was grossly inadequate. "T'an's conceptualization of the Ether," says the author, "was merely philosophical ornamentation which was absent in the Western constructs." Ether had nothing to do with electricity and the role of electricity in the functioning of the brain—as T'an presented it—was only a recent discovery which was unheard of in T'an's days. The author believes that it is a coincidence. (What a wonderful coincidence!) T'an's shortcomings in his scientific thought, the author says, can be ascribed to the difficulty of rendering English terms in Chinese, and this indicates the difficulty of communication between two cultures.

133 "T'an Fu-sheng shih-lüeh 譚復生事略 [A biographical sketch of T'an Ssu-t'ung]
In *Pao-hsüeh chi-k'an* 報學季刊 , Vol. 1, No. 1 (July 1934), p. 144.

Verbatim reprint of Liang's "Biography of T'an Ssu-t'ung."

134 T'an Hsün-ts'ung 譚訓聰, "Hsien tsu-mu (T'an Ssu-t'ung fu-jen) chia-chuan" 先祖母（譚嗣同夫人）家傳 [A family biography of my late grandmother Mrs. T'an Ssu-t'ung]
In *Hu-nan wen-hsien* 湖南文獻, Vols. 6 & 7 (Oct. 1972), p. 122.

This is perhaps the most reliable account of the life of Mrs. T'an of whom very little is known. It tells of the enthusiasm with which Mrs. T'an participated in the founding of the China Women's College 中國女子學堂 . After the death of T'an Ssu-t'ung, Mrs. T'an pressed for the setting up of a girls' school in Liuyang, of which she was director for ten years. In 1923, she was awarded a wooden tablet by the Chinese government with the inscription 巾幗完人 (A perfect woman). Mrs. T'an had two miscarriages, both girls. She gave birth to a boy who died at the age of one. T'an Hsün-ts'ung's father was the adopted son of T'an Ssu-t'ung. In the short "remarks", the author deplores the fact that many writers have distorted the true facts about Mrs. T'an, and hopes that this account can help to correct them.

135　T'an Hsün-ts'ung 譚訓聰 , "T'an Ssu-t'ung fu-jen shih-lüeh" 譚嗣同夫人事略 [A brief account of Mrs. T'an Ssu-t'ung]

In *I wen chih* 藝文誌 , Vol. 30 (March 1968), pp. 21-22.

The author, an adopted grandson of T'an Ssu-t'ung, subtitled his article " 爲先祖母李太恭人殉夫一事辨正 ". As the subtitle suggests, this article is a refutation of untruthful accounts of Mrs. T'an's committing suicide. He points out that Lin Kuang-ying's article follows Liang Ch'i-ch'ao's and therefore unfortunately repeats Liang's mistakes. To present a truthful account rather than rectifying what has been wrongly written by others, T'an Hsün-ts'ung reprints here his article of the above entry.

136　T'an Hsün-ts'ung 譚訓聰 , *Ssu-t'ung kung nien-p'u ch'u-kao* 嗣同公年譜初稿 [A draft chronological biography of my grandfather T'an Ssu-t'ung]

Mentioned by Huang Chang-chien in his *Wu-hsü pien-fa shih yen-ch'iu* 戊戌變法史研究 .

137　T'an P'i-mo 譚丕模 , *Ch'ing-tai ssu-hsiang shih-kang* 清代思想史綱 [A concise history of Ch'ing thought]

Shanghai: K'ai-ming shu-chü, 1940, pp. 105-115.

The author, by his special method of classification, places T'an under the heading of "Civilian thought" together with K'ang Yu-wei, Liang Ch'i-ch'ao, Chang Ping-lun 章炳麟 and Yen Fu 嚴復 . After a discussion of some of the ideas contained in the *Jen-hsüeh*, he concludes with a few remarks on T'an, praising him for "bursting through all enmeshing webs" and thinks this is the spirit of the revolutionary bourgeoise.

138 T'an P'i-mo 譚丕模 , "T'an Ssu-t'ung lun" 譚嗣同論 [On T'an Ssu-t'ung] In *Wen-hua p'i-p'an* 文化批判 , Vol. 4, No. 2 (April 1937), pp. 105-111.

Outlines the main tenets of the *Jen-hsüeh*.

139 T'an Ssu-t'ung 譚嗣同 , *Ch'iu-yü nien-hua chih kuan ts'ung-ts'uo shu* 秋雨年華之館叢脞書[Miscellaneous writings from the Ch'iu-yü nien-hua Studio]

Published by T'an in 1897, Ch'angsha, Hunan.

140 T'an Ssu-t'ung, "Ch'iu-yü nien-hua chih kuan ts'ung-ts'uo shu chung wei-k'an kao" 秋雨年華之館叢脞書中未刊稿[Unpublished materials in the *Miscellaneous writings from the Ch'iu-yü nien-hua Studio*]

In Hu-nan sheng-chih hsüeh-shu-chih pien-ch'i hsiao-tsu 湖南省志學術志編輯小組 (ed.), *Hu-nan li-shih tzu-liao* 湖南歷史資料 , Vol. 8 (Dec. 1959), pp. 113-138.

Collected here are the following:

"I-wei tai Lung Chih-sheng shih-lang tsou-ch'ing pien-t'ung k'o-chü hsien ts'ung sui-k'o-shih ch'i che" 乙未代龍芝生侍郎奏請變通科舉先從歲科試起折 [A memorial written in 1895 for Vice-Minister Lung Chan-lin 龍湛霖 , recommending a change in the civil examinations beginning with the annual candidacy examination]   pp. 113-115

" 'Kuan-yin piao' tzu-hsü" 「管音表」自敍 [Author's preface to "Musical scale for flute"]   pp. 115-117

"Huang Ying-ch'u 'Chuan-ying k'uai-tzu chien-fa' hsü" 黃穎初「傳音快字簡法」敍 [Preface to Huang Ying-ch'u's "A simple method of shorthand based on pronunciation"]   pp. 117-118

"Chin-ling ts'e-liang-hui chang-ch'eng" 金陵測量會章程 [Regulations of the Nanking Surveying Society]   pp. 118-120

"Ch'uang-pan 'K'uang-hsüeh-pao' kung-ch'i" 創辦「礦學報」公啟 [A public statement concerning the establishment of the *Mining News*]   pp. 120-122

" 'Nung-hsüeh hui' hui-yu pan-shih chang-ch'eng" 「農學會」會友辦事章程 [Regulations for members of the Agronomy Society regarding the management of society affairs]   pp. 122-124

"Yü T'ang Fu-ch'eng shu" 與唐紱丞書 [A letter to T'ang Ts'ai-ch'ang]
                                           pp. 124-126; pp. 126-130

"Yü Hsü Yen-fu shu" 與徐硯甫書 [A letter to Hsü Jen-chu 徐仁鑄]
                                           pp. 130-132

"Shang Ch'en Yu-ming fu-pu shu" 上陳右銘撫部書 [A letter to
    Governor-general Ch'en Pao-chien 陳寶箴]   pp. 132-135

"Pao T'u Chih-ch'u shu" 報涂質初書 [A letter in reply to T'u Ju-ho
    涂儒翯]   pp. 135-136

"Tseng Liang Lien-chien hsien-sheng hsü" 贈梁蓮澗先生序 [A preface
    to Mr. Liang Pao-ying 梁寶英]   pp. 137-138

141 **T'an Ssu-t'ung** *et al.* **(ed.),** *Hsiang-pao* 湘報 **[The Hunan Daily]**
     9th March, 1898 to 6th May, 1898.

     Details of T'an writings published in this newspaper are given below:

Title	*Issue*	*Date*	*Pages*
'T'an Fu-sheng kuan-ch'a ti-i-tz'u chiang i" 譚復生觀察第一次講義 [Notes of the first lecture given by Prefect T'an Ssu-t'ung]	3	9 Mar.	10a-10b
"Yen-nien-hui chang-ch'eng" 延年會章程 [Regulations of the Longevity Society]	4	10 Mar.	13a-14a
"T'an Fu-sheng kuan-ch'a Nan-hsüeh-hui ti-erh-tz'u chiang-i" 譚復生觀察南學會 第二次講義 [Notes of the second lecture given to the Nan-hsüeh Society by Prefect T'an Ssu-t'ung]	7	14 Mar.	25a-26b
"Shih-hsing yin-hua shui t'iao-shuo" 試行 印花稅條說 [A proposal to try out a stamp-duty law]	9 10	16 Mar. 17 Mar.	33a-33b 37a-37b
"Hsiang-pao hou-hsü" 湘報後敍 [Second preface to the *Hunan Daily*]	11	18 Mar.	41
"Kai-ping Liu-yang ch'eng hsiang ke shu-yüan wei chih-yung hsüeh-t'ang kung-ch'i" 改併瀏陽城鄉各書院爲致用學堂 公啟 [A public statement regarding a plan to convert academies of the various towns and villages of Liuyang county into schools of practical learning]	11	18 Mar.	42b-43a

"Tu Nan-hai K'ang kung-pu t'iao-ch'en
Chiao-shih che shu-hou" 讀南海康工部
條陳膠事折書後[Comments on K'ang
Yu-wei's memorial on the Chiao-chou
Incident]   16 24 Mar.   61a

"Lun Hsiang-Yüeh t'ieh-lu chih i" 論湘粵
鐵路之益 [A discussion of the advan-
tages of a Hunan-Kwangtung Railway]   19 28 Mar.   73a-74a

"T'an Fu-sheng kuan-ch'a Nan-hsüeh-hui
ti-wu-tz'u chiang-i" 譚復生觀察南學會
第五次講義 [Notes of the fifth lecture
given to the Nan-hsüeh Society by Pre-
fect T'an Ssu-t'ung]   20 29 Mar.   79a-79b

"Chi kuan-shen chi-i pao-wei-chu shih"記
官紳集議保衞局事 [An account of the
exchange of opinions between officials
and gentry on the establishment of a
bureau of local guards]   25 4 April   97a

"Lun tien-teng chih i" 論電燈之益 [A dis-
cussion of the advantages of electric
light]   29 8 April   113a-113b

"Ch'ün-meng hsüeh-hui hsü" 羣萌學會敍
[An Introduction to the Ch'ün-meng
Study Society]   32 12 April 125a-126a

"Chih-shih p'ien" 治事篇 [Essays on state-
craft] , No. 1-4.   35 15 April 137a-137b
No. 5-7   36 16 April 141a-141b
No. 8-10   37 18 April 145a-145b

"Yen-nien-hui   kao-pai" 延年會告白 [A
public notice of the Longevity Society]   40 21 April 160b

"T'an Fu-sheng kuan-ch'a Nan-hsüeh-hui
ti-pa-tz'u chiang-i 譚復生觀察南學會第
八次講義 [Notes of the eighth lecture
given to the Nan-hsüeh Society by Pre-
fect T'an Ssu-t'ung]   42 23 April 165a-166b

"I-t'ai shuo" 以太說 [An essay on Ether]   53 6 May   209a

"Hu-nan pu-ch'an-tsu-hui chia-ch'ü chang-
ch'eng" 湖南不纏足會嫁娶章程 [Regu-

lations regarding marriage drafted by
the Hunan Non-Footbinding Society]   53 6 May   212a

142 T'an Ssu-t'ung, "I-t'ai shuo" 以太說 [An essay on Ether]
In *Min-ch'üan su* 民權素, Vol. 5 (March 1915), pp. 2-4.

Other writings of T'an published in this journal include:

"Chung-shu Ssu-shu i tzu-hsü" 仲叔四書義自敍 [Author's preface to the
commentaries on the *Four Books* by my elder brother Ssu-hsiang
嗣襄 and Ssu-t'ung], *Min-ch'üan su* 民權素, Vol. 5 (March 1915),
pp. 5-6.

"Shih li tzu-hsü" 史例自敍 [Preface to the format of a history book],
ibid., Vol. 5 (March 1915), pp. 8-9.

"Hai-chiao fu-chün chia-chuan" 海崎府君家傳 [A family biography of
my ancester T'an Chi-sheng 譚繼昇], *ibid.*, Vol. 6 (May 1915), pp. 4-5.

"Chih-shih p'ien shih-ming tzu-hsü" 治事篇釋名自敍 [Author's preface
to the section "An explanation of names" in "Essays on statecraft"],
ibid., Vol. 6 (May 1915), pp. 6-7.

"Pao Tsou Yüeh-sheng shu" 報鄒岳生書 [A letter in reply to Tsou
Yüeh-sheng], *ibid.*, Vol. 6 (May 1915), pp. 10-11.

"Ch'ün-meng hsüeh-hui hsü" 羣萌學會敍 [Preface to the Ch'ün-meng
Study Society], *ibid.*, Vol. 7 (June 1915), pp. 7-8.

"Yüan-i-tang chi wai wen ch'u-p'ien tzu-hsü" 遠遺堂集外文初編自敍
[Editor's preface to the first supplement to (my elder brother's)
Collected Works of the Yüan-i Studio], *ibid.*, Vol. 8 (July 1915),
pp. 4-5.

"Yü Shen Hsiao-i shu" 與沈小沂書 [A letter to Shen Hsiáo-i], *ibid.*,
Vol. 9 (Aug. 1915), pp. 10-11.

143 T'an Ssu-t'ung, *Jen-hsüeh* 仁學 [The *Jen-hsüeh*]
In *Ch'ing-i pao* 清議報 (reproduced in Taipei: Cheng-wen chu-pan-
she, 1967), from January 1899 to December 1901.

Details of the publication of the *Jen-hsüeh* in *Ch'ing-i pao* are given
below. Pagination quoted as given by the publisher in Taiwan.

Volume	Date	Paragraph	Pages
2	2 January, 1899	1	117-120
3	12 January, 1899	2	183-184
		3	184-185

Volume	Date	Paragraph	Pages
4	22 January, 1899	3	205-212
		4	241
		5	241-242
		6	242-243
		7	243-244
		8	244-245
		9	246-248
5	1 February, 1899		303-304
		10	304-306
		11	306-308
		12	308-310
7	2 March, 1899		435
		13	435-436
		14	436-438
		15	438-440
9	22 March, 1899		563
		16	563-566
		17	566-568
		18	568
10	1 April, 1899		629-631
		19	631-634
		20	634
12	20 April, 1899		753-755
		21	755-757
		22	757-758
14	10 May, 1899		889
		23	890-891
		24	891-893
		25	893-894
44	9 May, 1900		2903-2906
		26	2906
45	19 May, 1900		2973
		27	2973-2975
		28	2975-2976
			3033
46	28 May, 1900	29	3035-3036
		30	3036-3038
		31	3038

47

Volume	Date	Paragraph	Pages
100	21 December, 1901		6441-6442
		32	6442-6444
		33	6444-6446
		34	6447-6449
		35	6449-6451
		36	6451-6453
		37	6453-6455
		38	6455-6458
		39	6458-6460
		40	6460-6461
		41	6461-6462
		42	6463-6470
		43	6470-6473
		44	6473-6476
		45	6476-6478
		46	6478-6481
		47	6481-6482
		48	6482-6483

144 T'an Ssu-t'ung, *Jen-hsüeh* 仁學 [The *Jen-hsüeh*]
In *Ch'ing-i pao ch'üan-p'ien* 清議報全篇 , Yokohama: Hsin-min she, n.d.

145 T'an Ssu-t'ung, *Jen-hsüeh* 仁學 [The *Jen-hsüeh*]
Shanghai: Chung-hua shu-chü, 1958. 83 pages.

146 T'an Ssu-t'ung, *Jen-hsüeh* 仁學 [The *Jen-hsüeh*]
Taipei: Ta-chung shu-chü, 1958. 88 pages.

147 T'an Ssu-t'ung, *Jen-hsüeh* 仁學 [The *Jen-hsüeh*]
Tokyo: Kuo-min pao-she ch'u-yang hsüeh-sheng pien-i-so, 1911.

148 **T'an Ssu-t'ung, "Liu-yang hsing-suan chi" 瀏陽興算記 [An account of the promotion of the learning of mathematics in Liuyang, Hunan]**
In Hu-nan sheng-chih hsüeh-shu-chih pien-chi hsiao-tsu 湖南省志學術志編輯小組 (ed.), *Hu-nan li-shih tzu-liao* 湖南歷史資料 , Vol. 6 (July 1959), pp. 159-174.

The article is printed in full here.

149 **T'an Ssu-t'ung, *T'an Liu-yang ch'üan-chi* 譚瀏陽全集 [Collected works of T'an Ssu-t'ung of Liuyang]**

Edited by Ch'en Nai-ch'ien 陳乃乾. Shanghai: Wen-ming ch'u-pan-she, 1952. Reprinted in Taipei: Wen-hai ch'u-pan-she, 1962.

As stated in the preface, the editor compiled this volume because Liang Ch'i-ch'ao did not compile *T'an Ssu-t'ung i-chi* 譚嗣同遺集 as promised in his biography of T'an. This volume includes first, a chrono-logical biography by Ch'en Nai-ch'ien; second, a collection of articles and a few letters of T'an, and some of the biographies T'an wrote; third, T'an's poems written before the age of thirty; fourth, a complete version of the *Jen-hsüeh*, and lastly, two volumes of the "Miscellaneous Notes". The writings included in this volume are drawn mainly from the *Hsiang-pao* 湘報 and the *Shih-wu pao* 時務報.

150 T'an Ssu-t'ung, "T'an Liu-yang i-mo" 譚瀏陽遺墨 [A piece of posthu-mous writing by T'an Ssu-t'ung of Liuyang]
    In Liang Ch'i-ch'iao 梁啟超, *Yin-ping-shih ch'üan-chi* 飲冰室全集 [Complete works of the Ice-drinking Studio]. Shanghai: Chung-hua shu-chü, 1916, Vol. 42, pp. 37a-38a.

A piece of writing by T'an, possibly done after the composition of the *Jen-hsüeh*. Included in *TSTCC* as "I-mo san-p'ien" 遺墨三篇 (*TSTCC*, pp. 280-281).

151 T'an Ssu-t'ung, *T'an Ssu-t'ung chen-chi* 譚嗣同眞蹟 [Authentic auto-graphs of T'an Ssu-t'ung]
    Compiled by Wen Ts'ao 文操. Shanghai: Shang-hai ch'u-pan-kung-ssu, 1955.

Contains autographs of T'an, mainly letters with a few poems. Some omissions from *TSTCC* are added here.

152 T'an Ssu-t'ung, *T'an Ssu-t'ung chi* 譚嗣同集 [Collected writings of T'an Ssu-t'ung]
    Shanghai: Ch'ün-hsüeh she, 1927, 2 vols.

153 T'an Ssu-t'ung, "T'an Ssu-t'ung Ch'iu-yü nien-hua chih kuan ts'ung-ts'uo shu (kao-pan) hsüan-k'an" 譚嗣同秋雨年華之館叢脞書(稿本)選刊 [Selected sections from the draft of T'an Ssu-t'ung's *Miscellaneous Writings from the Ch'iu-yü nien-hua Studio*]
    In Hu-nan sheng-chih hsüeh-shu-chih pien-chi hsiao-tsu 湖南省志學術志編輯小組 (ed.), *Hu-nan li-shih tzu-liao* 湖南歷史資料, Vol. 9 (March 1960), pp. 95-101.

Collected here are the following:

"Chih-shih p'ien" 治事篇 [Essays on statecraft]   pp. 95-97

"Tu Nan-hai K'ang kung-pu t'iao-ch'en Chiao-shih che shu-hou 讀南海康
工部條陳膠事折書後 [Comments on K'ang Yu-wei's memorial on
the Chiao-chou Incident]   p. 97

"Chin-ling t'ing-fa shih chu" 金陵聽法詩註 [Annotation to the poem
"Receiving instructions on Buddhism in Nanking"]   pp. 97-98

"Sung Wu Yen-chou hsien-sheng kuan Kuei-chou shih hsü" 送吳雁舟先生
官貴州詩紋 [Preface to the poem presented to Mr. Wu Chia-jui 嘉瑞
on his departure to his official appointment in Kuei-chou]   p. 98

"Fa-jen wu-ku so Tien pien Wu-wu-ti, ching-chieh chih, huo wei-chih
yao" 法人無故索滇邊烏烏地，竟界之，或爲之謠 [A ditty on the
French who unreasonably demanded the district of Meng-wu Wu-te
猛烏烏得 in Yünnan and even made it their dominion]   p. 98

"T'i Ku Shih-kung so pien Ku-shih chung-chen lu chien ta ch'i chien-
tseng-shih" 題顧石公所編顧氏忠貞錄兼答其見贈詩 [Writing a poem
on A Family History of the Kus, edited by Ku Yün 顧雲, as a reply
to the poem he presented to me]   p. 98

"Chi T'ang Fu-ch'eng shih" 寄唐紱丞詩 [A poem to T'ang Ts'ai-ch'ang
唐才常]   p. 98

"T'i Ch'eng Tzu-ta heng-lan t'u shih" 題程子大橫覽圖詩 [A poem on
Ch'eng Sung-wan's 程頌萬 [panoramic landscape painting]   p. 99

"Chi ti Ch'in-sheng shih" 寄弟秦生詩 [A poem to my younger brother
T'an Ssu-chiung 譚嗣囧]   p. 99

"T'i Chiang Chien-hsia 'Tung lin ch'iao hsiao t'u' shih" 題江建霞東鄰巧
笑圖詩 [A poem on Chiang Piao's 江標 painting, "Charming smiles
from the eastern neighbour"]   p. 99

"Sung Chiang Chien-hsia kuei Su-chou shih" 送江建霞歸蘇州詩 [Seeing
off Chiang Piao on his return to Su-chou]   p. 99

"Mo-ch'ou hu lien-yü" 莫愁湖聯語 [A couplet written at Lake Mo-
ch'ou]   p. 100

"Ta-hsien Wu Ch'iao ssu yü Hu-pei, chi fu Chi-ch'ing hsien-sheng chih-
hsien Ch'ien-t'ang, yin tsang chu Hsi-hu chih shang, Hsin-hui Liang
Ch'i-ch'ao ming chih yüeh 'T'ien-min Wu Ch'iao chih mu', Ssu-t'ung
chiang wang hui tsang, erh ai i lien-yü" 達縣吳樵死於湖北其父季清先
生知縣錢塘因葬諸西湖之上新會梁啓超銘之曰天民吳樵之墓嗣同將往
會葬而哀以聯語 [A couplet to lament, before attending the funeral,

50

Wu Ch'iao of Ta County, Szechuan. Wu died in Hupei, but his father, Mr. Wu Te-su 吳德潚, who is the District Magistrate of Hang-chou, has him buried in the Western Lake. Liang Ch'i-ch'ao of Hsin-hui, Kwangtung, inscribed the words "The Tomb of Wu Ch'iao of Sze-chuan" on the tombstone]   p. 100

"Chih Liu Chü-hsing shu i" 致劉聚卿書一 [Letter to Liu Shih-heng 劉世珩, No. 1]   pp. 100-101

"Chih Liu Chü-hsing shu erh" 致劉聚卿書二 [Letter to Liu Shih-heng, No. 2]   p. 101

154 **T'an Ssu-t'ung, *T'an Ssu-t'ung ch'üan-chi* 譚嗣同全集 [Complete works of T'an Ssu-t'ung]**

Edited by Ts'ai Shang-ssu 蔡尚思. Peking: San-lien shu-tien, 1954. 534 pages.

The best collection of T'an's writings. Particularly important is the fine collection of hitherto unpublished personal correspondence of T'an from various sources. The editor has rearranged T'an's work into four parts: (1) political and social essays; (2) descriptive essays; (3) personal correspondence; (4) poems and rhymed proses. In the appendix, four other writings are included. They are: "*Jen-hsüeh* hsü" 仁學序 by Liang Ch'i-ch'ao, "Shang Ou-yang Pan-chiang shih shu hsü" 上歐陽瓣薑師書序 by Ou-yang Yü-ch'ien 歐陽予倩, "T'an Ssu-t'ung chuan" 譚嗣同傳 by Liang Ch'i-ch'ao and "Liu-ai shih" 六哀詩 by K'ang Yu-wei. In using this volume, one has to be careful about the punctuation which is often arbitrary. Three poems, "Shu-huai shih" 述懷詩 on pp. 451, 475 and, "Tseng Ch'iu Wen-chieh" 贈邱文階 on p. 475 are believed to be the works of T'an Ssu-hsiang 譚嗣襄, and not of Ssu-t'ung. This volume, moreover, has to be supplemented with materials provided in the *Hu-nan li-shih tzu-liao* 湖南歷史資料 and Wen Ts'ao's 文操 *T'an Ssu-t'ung chen-chi* 譚嗣同眞蹟 where there is a supplement to the omissions in this volume, made possible by the availability of the whole set of the *Hsiang pao* 湘報.

155 **T'an Ssu-t'ung, "T'an Ssu-t'ung i-kao" 譚嗣同佚稿 [Missing letters of T'an Ssu-t'ung]**

In Hu-nan sheng-chih hsüeh-shu-chih pien-chi hsiao-tsu 湖南省志學術志編輯小組 (ed.), *Hu-nan li-shih tzu-liao* 湖南歷史資料, Vol. 4 (Dec. 1958), pp. 58-64.

Included here are six letters T'an wrote to Liu Sung-fu (Shan-han) 劉淞芙（善涵）.

156 **T'an Ssu-t'ung, "T'an Ssu-t'ung i-mo hsü-k'an"** 譚嗣同遺墨續刊 **[Further publication of the unpublished letters of T'an Ssu-t'ung]**
In Hu-nan sheng-chih hsüeh-shu-chih pien-chi hsiao-tsu 湖南省志學術志編輯小組 (ed.), *Hu-nan li-shih tzu-liao* 湖南歷史資料 , Vol. 5 (March 1959), pp. 76-79.

It includes:

"Chih fu-jen shu i" 致夫人書一 [Letter to my wife, No. 1]   p. 76
"Chih fu-jen shu erh" 致夫人書二 [Letter to my wife, No. 2] pp. 76-77
"Chih Tsou Yüeh-sheng shu" 致鄒岳生書 [A letter to Tsou Yüeh-sheng]   p. 77
"Shang ta po-fu-mu shu i" 上大伯父母書一 [Letter to my father's eldest brother and his wife, No. 1]   p. 77
"Shang ta po-fu-mu shu erh" 上大伯父母書二 [Letter to my father's eldest brother and his wife, No. 2]   p. 78
"Shang ta po-fu-mu shu san" 上大伯父母書三 [Letter to my father's eldest brother and his wife, No. 3]   p. 78
"Shang ta po-fu-mu shu ssu" 上大伯父母書四 [Letter to my father's eldest brother and his wife, No. 4]   pp. 78-79

157 **T'an Ssu-t'ung, *T'an Ssu-t'ung shu-chien*** 譚嗣同書簡 **[Letters of T'an Ssu-t'ung]**
Edited by Ou-yang Yü-ch'ien 歐陽予倩 . Shanghai: Wen-hua kung-ying she, 1948.

See separate entry under "Ou-yang Yü-ch'ien".

158 **T'an Ssu-t'ung, "T'an Ssu-t'ung wei-k'an i-kao"** 譚嗣同未刊遺稿 **[Unpublished writings of T'an Ssu-t'ung]**
In *Chung-kuo chien-she yüeh-k'an* 中國建設月刊 ,Vol. 4, No. 3 (June 1947), pp. 54-57.

Includes two pieces by T'an viz. "Pei-yu fang-hsüeh chi" 北遊訪學記 and "Shang Ou-yang Pan-chiang shih shu" 上歐陽瓣薑師書 (No. 28 in *TSTCC*).

159 **T'an Ssu-t'ung, "T'an Ssu-t'ung wei-k'an shou-cha"** 譚嗣同未刊手札 **[Unpublished letters of T'an Ssu-t'ung]**
In Hu-nan sheng-chih hsüeh-shu-chih pien-chi hsiao-tsu 湖南省志學術志編輯小組 (ed.), *Hu-nan li-shih tzu-liao* 湖南歷史資料 , Vol. 3 (July 1958), pp. 77-78.

Includes:

"Chih Chi Yün shu" 致齎雲書 [A letter to Chi Yün]   pp. 77-78

"Chih fu-jen shu" 致夫人書 [A letter to my wife]   p. 78

160 T'an Ssu-t'ung, *Tung-hai Ch'ien-ming shih san-shih i-ch'ien chiu-hsüeh*
東海褰冥氏三十以前舊學[The writings of T'an Ssu-t'ung before the age
of thirty]
Nanking: Chin-ling yin-shu-kuan, 1897.

161 T'an Ssu-t'ung, "Wen Hsin-kuo kung Chiao-yü ch'in chi chen-chi" 文信
國公蕉雨琴記眞蹟 [Authentic autograph of "An account of the revered
Wen Tien-hsiang's Chiao-yü lute"]
In Chou K'ang-hsieh 周康燮 (ed.), *Chung-kuo chin san-pai-nien
hsüeh-shu ssu-hsiang lun-chi erh-pien* 中國近三百年學術思想論集二編
[Second collection of articles on Chinese learning and thought of the
last three hundred years]. Hong Kong: Ch'ung-wen shu-tien, 1971,
pp. 249-250.

This scroll is owned by Mr. Chou's mother. Reproduced here in
fascimile.

162 T'an Ssu-t'ung and Chang Ping-lin 章炳麟 , *Chang T'an ho ch'ao* 章譚合
鈔 [Works of Chang Ping-lin and T'an Ssu-t'ung]
Shanghai: Kuo-hsüeh fu-lan she, 1910. Reprinted in Taipei: Kuang-
wen shu-tien, 1977.

Contains 96 pages of T'an's writings in two *chüan*. Taken mainly
from *Tung-hai Ch'ien-ming shih san-shih i-ch'ien chiu-hsüeh* 東海褰冥氏
三十以前舊學 and a few paragraphs from "Shih-chü ying-lu pi-chih"
石菊影廬筆識 .

163 T'an Ssu-t'ung and T'ang Ts'ai-ch'ang 唐才常 , *Liu-yang erh-chieh i-wen*
瀏陽二傑遺文 [The posthumous writings of the two heroes of Liuyang,
Hunan]
2 vols. n.d. & n.p.

164 T'an Ssu-t'ung and T'ang Ts'ai-ch'ang, *T'an Fu-sheng T'ang Fo-ch'en
hsien-sheng mo-chi* 譚復生唐佛塵先生墨跡 [Manuscripts of Messrs. T'an
Ssu-t'ung and T'ang Ts'ai-ch'ang]
Shanghai: Hsüan-ho yin-she, n.d.

165 T'an Ssu-t'ung and T'ang Ts'ai-ch'ang, "T'an Fu-sheng T'ang Fo-ch'en i-kao" 譚復生唐佛塵遺稿 [Posthumous works of T'an Ssu-t'ung and T'ang Ts'ai-ch'ang]

In *Ch'ing-ho* 青鶴 , Vol. 5, No. 1 (Nov. 1936), pp. 1-5; No. 3 (Dec. 1936), pp. 1-4; No. 5 (Jan. 1937), pp. 1-3; No. 7 (Feb. 1937), pp. 1-4; No. 9 (March 1937), pp. 1-4; No. 11 (April 1937), pp. 1-2.

Reprinted here in alternate issues is T'an's "Shang Ou-yang Pan-chiang shih shu erh-shih-erh" 上歐陽瓣薑師書二十二 [Letter to my teacher Ou-yang Chung-ku, No. 22]. See *TSTCC*, pp. 316-329.

166 T'ang Chih-chün 湯志鈞 , "Jen-hsüeh pan-pen t'an-yüan" 仁學版本探源 [Tracing the source of the editions of the *Jen-hsüeh*]

In *Hsüeh-shu yüeh-kan* 學術月刊 , Vol. 5 (May 1963).

The author believes that the versions of the *Jen-hsüeh* published by *Ch'ing-i pao* in Yokohama and *Ya-tung shih-pao* 亞東時報 in Shanghai had many differences because they were not based on one original draft: the former was based on Liang Ch'i-ch'ao's copy, the latter on T'ang Ts'ai-ch'ang's. Kuo-min pao-she 國民報社 was the first to publish the work separately, based on the copy owned by Liang Ch'i-ch'ao. For future re-editing of the text of the *Jen-hsüeh*, the author suggests that it should be based on the *Ya-tung shih-pao's* version because (1) it was more reliable; (2) it apparently had not been tampered with as the *Ch'ing-i pao* and Kuo-ming pao-she texts had been. Furthermore, many examples attest to the lucid and logical structure of the text of the *Jen-hsüeh*. Nevertheless, the *Ya-tung shih-pao* version has to be further collated with other versions because (1) it is not the original draft and misprints are often found; (2) blank brackets may be filled up by comparing them with other versions; (3) the respective versions of *Ch'ing-i pao* and *Ya-tung shih-pao* came from the same original draft.

167 T'ang Chih-chün 湯志鈞 , *Wu-hsü pien-fa jen-wu chuan-kao* 戊戌變法人物傳稿 [Draft biographies of important figures in the 1898 Reform Movement]

Peking: Chung-hua shu-chü, 1961, pp. 29-40.

A much more elaborate version than Liang's biography. The author makes good use of T'an's material recently published in the *Hu-nan li-shih tzu-liao*. Particularly useful are two "chüeh-ming shu" 絕命書 not included in *TSTTC*, which were originally published in *Chih-hsin pao* 知新報 .

168 Teng Ssu-yü 鄧嗣禹 , "T'an Ssu-t'ung"

In Arthur W. Hummel *et al., Eminent Chinese of the Ch'ing Period, 1644-1912*. Washington, D.C.: United States Government Printing Office, 1943-1944, pp. 702-705.

A well-balanced, concise account of the life of T'an, without, however, much discussion of his thought.

169 **Teng Ssu-yü and John K. Fairbank** *et al., China's Response to the West: A Documentary Survey, 1839-1923*

Cambridge, Mass.: Harvard University Press, 1954, pp. 157-160.

The author describes T'an as a "precocious and ingenious thinker, and an emotional and heroic young man of high principles." He then introduces T'an's ideas in the *Jen-hsüeh*, adding that "almost alone in 1898 he favored China's 'complete Westernization' (*ch'üan-pan hsi-hua* 全盤西化) and the abandonment or remaking of Confucianism and traditional culture." Excerpts from "Pao Pei Yüan-cheng shu" 報貝元徵書 are translated here to give readers a glimpse of T'an's thought.

170 **Ts'ai Kuan-lo** 蔡冠洛 **(ed. & comp.),** *Ch'ing-tai ch'i-pai ming-jen chuan* 清代七百名人傳 **[Biographies of seven hundred prominent figures of the Ch'ing dynasty]**

Originally printed in 1936, reprinted in Hong Kong: Yüan-tung t'u-shu kung-ssu, 1963, pp. 1911-1913.

A verbatim reprint of Liang's biography.

171 **Ts'ai Shang-ssu** 蔡尚思 , **"T'an Ssu-t'ung hsüeh-shu ssu-hsiang t'i-yao"** 譚嗣同學術思想提要 **[The essentials of T'an Ssu-t'ung's learning and thought]**

In *Chung-kuo chien-she* 中國建設 , Vol. 2, No. 2 (May 1947), pp. 49-53.

The author praises T'an's bravery which he thinks was a result of (1) his misfortunes in childhood; (2) his belief in the altruistic principles of Mo Tzu; and (3) his forthright character. In thought, T'an is regarded by this author as a "vanguard" and a "bombshell" of the late Ch'ing intellectual world: vanguard, because the thought expressed in the *Jen-hsüeh* was far more advanced than K'ang Yu-wei's *Ta-t'ung shu* 大同書 and the revolutionary ideas of the Tung-meng hui 同盟會 ; bombshell, because of his iconoclastic idea of "breaking out of all enmeshing nets".

T'an's thought, moreover, was "complete Westernization" and not, as Liang Ch'i-ch'ao once remarked in his *Ch'ing-tai hsüeh-shu k'ai-lun* 清代學術概論, "neither East nor West." T'an was only paying lip-service to Confucianism. The author then proceeds to analyse both the good and bad sides of T'an's philosophical, political, social, economic, religious and scholastic thinking. His main shortcoming, the author points out, was the stark contradictions in his thought. In comparing T'an with Chang Ping-lin 章炳麟, the former saw the loopholes of the feudal society and leant towards capitalism, the latter excelled at pinpointing the shortcomings of a capitalistic society but inclined to a feudalistic one. As to the literary achievement of T'an, the author thinks that T'an was liberal in the composition of poems but somewhat conservative in his euphuistically antithetic writing style. The article ends with a discussion of T'an's extant works.

172 **Tso Shun-sheng** 左舜生, **"T'an, Huang, Sung, Ts'ai ssu hsien-sheng p'ing-chuan"**譚、黃、宋、蔡四先生評傳**[Interpretative biographies of T'an Ssu-t'ung, Huang Hsing** 黃興 **, Sung Chiao-jen** 宋教仁 **and Ts'ai E** 蔡鍔 **]**
   In *Hsien-tai tsa-chih* 現代雜誌 , Vol. 1, No. 1 (Feb. 1965), pp. 37-41; No. 2 (March 1965), pp. 47-51; No. 3 (April 1965), pp. 42-46; No. 4 (May 1965), pp. 48-54.
   Reprinted in the author's *Chung-kuo chin-tai shih hua ch'u-chi* 中國近代史話初集 [Talks on modern Chinese history, Volume 1]. Hong Kong: Wen-i shu-wu, 1969, pp. 55-108.

   A lucid but sometimes digressive account of T'an.

173 **Tso Shun-sheng** 左舜生, **"T'an Ssu-t'ung hsien-sheng p'ing-chuan"** 譚嗣同先生評傳 **[An interpretative biography of Mr. T'an Ssu-t'ung]**
   In *Hu-nan wen-hsien* 湖南文獻 , Vol. 6, No. 1 (Jan. 1978), pp. 39-54.

   A reprint of the above article with very minor changes in wording.

174 **Tso Shun-sheng** 左舜生, **"T'an Ssu-t'ung p'ing-chuan"** 譚嗣同評傳 **[An interpretative biography of T'an Ssu-t'ung]**
   In *I wen chih* 藝文誌 , Vol. 19 (April 1967), pp. 4-11; Vol. 20 (May 1967), pp. 22-27; Vol. 21 (June 1967), pp. 19-21.

   A reprint of the author's article in *Hsien-tai tsa-chih* 現代雜誌 in 1965.

175 **Tung Ni** 冬尼, **"Kuan-yü T'an Ssu-t'ung pien-fa ssu-hsiang te pu-ch'ung**

i-chien" 關於譚嗣同變法思想的補充意見 [**Further ideas on the reformist thought of T'an Ssu-t'ung**]

In *Kuang-ming jih-pao* 光明日報 , 3rd March, 1955.

A comment on Cheng Ho-sheng's 鄭鶴聲 article. The author thinks that Cheng over-emphasizes the influence of the Neo-Confucianists such as Wang Fu-chih without paying due tribute to later figures like Yen Fu 嚴復 .

176 **Wang Chi** 忘機 , **"T'an Ssu-t'ung i-shih chih mi"** 譚嗣同遺詩之迷 [**The enigma in T'an Ssu-t'ung's posthumous poem**]

In *T'ien-wen-t'ai* 天文台 , No. 976 (4th April, 1956).

177 **Wang Chüeh** 王爝 , **"Ti-kuo chu-i nu-ts'ai te tsui-lien"** 帝國主義奴才的 嘴臉 [**The face of a lackey of imperialism**]

In *Kuei-chou jih-pao* 貴州日報 , 1st November, 1973.

Severely criticizes Ch'en Po-ta's article "Lun T'an Ssu-t'ung" which was written in 1933. The author lashes out at Ch'en's view that capitalism had greatly helped in the revitalization of China's economy in the later part of the nineteenth century.

178 **Wang Hsin-chien** 王心健 **"T'an Ssu-t'ung pu-tso ta-ko"** 譚嗣同不做大哥 [**T'an Ssu-t'ung did not want to be the head of a secret society**]

In *Chung-hua jih-pao* 中華日報 , 30th November, 1961, p. 8.

179 **Wang Huan-chih** 王煥之 , **"T'an Ssu-t'ung ch'üan-chi ch'u-pan"** 譚嗣同 全集出版 [**The publication of the *Complete Works of T'an Ssu-t'ung***]

In *Kuang-ming jih-pao* 光明日報 , 20th May, 1954.

Introduces T'an's thought and the contents of the *Complete Works*.

180 **Wang Teh-chao** 王德昭 , **"T'an Ssu-t'ung and the Political Movement of the Late Ch'ing Period"**

In Lawrence G. Thompson (ed.), *Studia Asiatica: Essays in Asian Studies in Felicitation of the Seventy-fifth Anniversary of Professor Ch'en Shou-yi*. San Francisco: Chinese Materials Center, Inc., 1975, pp. 125-155.

This article was originally presented as a paper to the Chinese Studies Section of the 29th International Congress of Orientalists at Paris during July 16th to 22nd, 1973. It is included in this volume almost as it was presented to the Congress, with only a few minor changes in footnotes. The author, making use of his profound knowledge of the intellectual history of the 1890s, sheds light on the wide ramifications of T'an's ideas and deeds on the development of politics in the late Ch'ing and early Republican period. What distinguishes this article from the rest of the present volume is its meticulously documented sources, its masterly use of Japanese writings, and above all, its keen historical insight into the significance of T'an in the germination of the concept of regional self-government, the intricate links T'an had with the secret societies and the traceable influence T'an bore upon revolutionaries of the pre-1911 period. The author offers some very acute comments on the various problematic issues related to T'an Ssu-t'ung, which, seen from the light of present scholarship, can be regarded almost as conclusive. The author believes that T'an was a leading figure in the Hunan Reform Movement because of his native social links, his better-than-average knowledge of the West, and above all, his being the first to initiate the idea of regional self-government—as can be seen by comparing the texts of T'an's "Shang Ou-yang Pan-chiang shih shu erh" (dated June 1895) and Liang's letter to Ch'en Po-chen (written in December 1897). The author also argues that the idea of urging the participation of gentry-literati in local government was first proposed by T'an as early as summer 1897. In the Hundred Days Reform, T'an was the most active in initiating the reopening of the Mou-ch'in Hall 懋勤殿, which was crucial for the maintenance of power in the hands of the reformers. The project, albeit abortive, was indicative of the important role T'an played in the reform.

T'an also had a profound influence on the late Ch'ing political movement. First, his martyrdom made him an idol of the Pao-huang hui 保皇會, the members of which formed the nucleus of the Uprising of 1900. The author also suspects that T'an, in his capacity as leader of a political movement, could have made advances to the secret societies earlier than any of his fellow compatriots, and thus first induced the forces of the secret societies of central China to enter into the political movement of that time. As for T'an's direct influence on the revolutionary activities leading to the Revolution of 1911, the *Jen-hsüeh* had three concepts influential to the revolutionaries: (1) the attack on the Hunan Army for their ruthless suppression of the Taipings; (2) the idea that it is only legitimate to die for a cause, not for the emperor; and (3) the necessity of shedding one's blood for the salvation of China; the impact of the last idea was borne out by four revolutionaries, Shen

Chin 沈藎, Yü Chih-mo 禹之謨, Yang Tu-sheng 楊篤生 and Wu Yüeh 吳樾.

181 **Wang Teh-chao** 王德昭, **"T'an Ssu-t'ung te kai-ke ssu-hsiang"** 譚嗣同的
改革思想 **[The reformist thought of T'an Ssu-t'ung]**
In *Hsin-ya hsüeh-sheng pao* 新亞學生報, February 1974, p. 3.

A lecture given to the students of New Asia College, The Chinese
University of Hong Kong. A summary introduction to the main politi-
cal ideas of T'an. Lucid and cogent.

182 **Wang Teh-chao** 王德昭, **"T'an Ssu-t'ung yü wan-Ch'ing cheng-chih yün-
tung"** 譚嗣同與晚清政治運動 **[T'an Ssu-t'ung and the political move-
ment of the late Ch'ing period]**
In *Journal of The Chinese University of Hong Kong*, Vol. 2, No. 1
(1974), pp. 33-69.

A much more detailed rendering in Chinese of the ideas already
expressed in the paper presented to the 29th International Congress of
Orientalists in 1973 (see item 180). The English summary of the article
is included here for reference:

"T'an Ssu-t'ung (1865-1898), a martyr of the Hundred Days'
Reform Movement of 1898, made only a fleeting appearance on the
stage of political activities from 1897 to 1898, but the role he played in
history is striking and his influence immense. He was one of the key
inspirers of a reform movement in his native province of Hunan, which
was the forerunner of the Hundred Days' Reform Movement, and became
its fighter and promoter when it was at its apogee in 1897-1898. He was
serving in the central government in Peking in September 1898, the last
stage of the Hundred Days, and became the Emperor's partisan in the
struggle for power at the imperial court. He was responsible for the
more drastic steps taken in these last days of the Reform Movement,
including the attempt to recruit Yüan Shih-k'ai for military support to
the cause of the Emperor.

"T'an, an anti-Manchu radical at heart, thus became a royalist and
died a martyr to a Manchu Emperor's cause. When the Royalists fled
and started the Emperor Protection Movement abroad, T'an became the
idol of the Royalists and was given the greatest publicity in their
publications.

"However, T'an also inspired young intellectuals of his time with
radicalism. Radicals like Lin Kuei, Shen Chin, Chou Jung, Wu Yüeh and

Yang Duh [Tu]-sheng were undoubtedly influenced by both his thought and his martyrdom.

"Finally, T'an's contact with secret societies of Hunan and Hupei probably also initiated a move which led to their participation first in the Royalists' uprising of 1900 and then in the revolutionary movement which ultimately overthrew the Manchu government."

183 **Wei Cheng-t'ung** 韋政通, *Chung-kuo che-hsüeh ssu-hsiang p'i-p'an* 中國 哲學思想批判 **[A critical account of the Chinese philosophical thought]**
Taipei: Shui-niu ch'u-pan-she, 1968, pp. 211-222.

The author attempts to look into the treatment T'an gave to some of the major philosophical concepts. He points out that T'an was probably wrong in his understanding of the concepts he criticized.

184 **Wen Ts'ao** 文操, *T'an Ssu-t'ung chen-chi* 譚嗣同眞蹟 **[Original manuscripts of T'an Ssu-t'ung]**
Shanghai: Shang-hai ch'u-pan-she, 1955. 166 pages.

Contains several photos of T'an, his studio, his friends, his grave, and above all, his original letters in fascimile. Also included here is a supplement to *T'an Ssu-t'ung ch'üan-chi*. For with the availability of the complete set of the *Hsiang Pao* 湘報, some omissions can be supplemented with new findings. A letter T'an wrote to Liang Ch'i-ch'ao is also found in Ti P'ing-tzu 狄平子, *P'ing-teng ko pi-chi* 平等閣筆記, *ch'üan* 4, p. 20, and printed here as an additional reference.

185 **Wile, D. David, "T'an Ssu-t'ung: His Life and Major Work, The *Jen-hsüeh*"**
Unpublished Ph.D. thesis of The University of Wisconsin, 1972. 610 pages.

This long and well-written doctoral thesis was supervised by Professor Chow Tse-tsung 周策縱. It has 2 parts in 7 chapters. Part 1 is "Biography" in which the writer adopts a chronological-and-interpretative approach to give a year-by-year account of the events and activities in T'an's life, while at the same time outlining the development of T'an's thought and major formative influences. Part 2 discusses terms, concepts, themes and topics found in the *Jen-hsüeh* so that a more integral picture of T'an's system can be seen. Virtually all important concepts are discussed in this part. In his presentation, apart from many sections translated from T'an's original writings, the writer also includes excerpts and summaries of representative minor works, supplementing them with the comments of T'an's contemporaries and later historians for amplification and perspective. No "conclusion" chapter, however, is included.

186 **Wu-chiu Chung-tzu** 沃邱仲子 (**Fei Hsing-chien** 費行簡), **"T'an Ssu-t'ung"** 譚嗣同 [**T'an Ssu-t'ung**]
In *Chin-tai ming-jen hsiao-chuan* 近代名人小傳 [Short biographies of personalities in modern China]. Taipei: Kuo-min ch'u-pan-she, 1955, pp. 353-354.

Merely a three-line introduction of T'an.

187 **Wu K'ang** 吳康 , *Chung-kuo hsien-tai che-hsüeh ch'u-pien* 中國現代哲學初編 [**First collection of articles on modern Chinese philosophy**]
Taipei: Cheng-chung shu-chü, 1975, pp. 55-67.

Factual and trite, glut with quotations. The only "novel" idea seems to be that the idea of Ether bears close resemblance to Anaxagoras' *nous*, the validity of which is highly dubious.

188 **Wu K'un-ju** 鄔昆如 **and Li Chien-ch'iu** 黎建球 , **"T'an Ssu-t'ung"** 譚嗣同 [**T'an Ssu-t'ung**]
In *Chung-hsi liang-pai-wei che-hsüeh-chia* 中西兩百位哲學家 [Two hundred Chinese and Western philosophers]. Taipei: Tung-ta tu-shu yu-hsien kung-ssu, 1978, pp. 323-324.

A summary of T'an's philosophy.

189 **Wu Liu-wu** 吳柳梧 , **"T'an Ssu-t'ung yü chiang-hu hsieh-shih"** 譚嗣同與江湖俠士 [**T'an Ssu-t'ung and his relationship with the wandering swordsmen**]
In *Ch'ang-liu* 暢流 , Vol. 39, No. 10 (July 1960), pp. 16-17.

Describes how T'an had contacts with gallant swordsmen. The article also makes the point that T'an had connections with the secret societies.

190 **Yang Cheng-tien** 楊正典 , **"T'an Ssu-t'ung ssu-hsiang yen-chiu"** 譚嗣同思想研究 [**A study of the thought of T'an Ssu-t'ung**]
In *Kuang-ming jih-pao* 光明日報 , 3rd and 17th November, 1954.

Possibly the first article on T'an after the publication of the *TSTCC*. It analyses the social background and logical presuppositions of his ideas, and gives a detailed analysis of T'an's thought. The author follows Ch'en Po-ta in asserting that T'an was basically a materialist.

191 **Yang Cheng-tien** 楊正典 , *T'an Ssu-t'ung—chin-tai Chung-kuo ch'i-meng ssu-hsiang-chia* 譚嗣同——近代中國啟蒙思想家 [T'an Ssu-t'ung **—an enlightenment thinker in modern China**]
Wuhan: Hu-pei jen-min ch'u-pan-she, 1955.

An enlarged and revised version of the last article.

192 **Yang I-feng** 楊一峯 , "T'an Ssu-t'ung" 譚嗣同 [T'an Ssu-t'ung]
In Chang Ch'i-chün 張其昀 *et al.* (ed.), *Chung-kuo wen-hsüeh shih lun-chi* 中國文學史論集 [An anthology of essays on the history of Chinese literature]. Taipei: Chung-hua wen-hua ch'u-pan shih-yeh-she, 1958, pp. 1169-1181.

Discusses the poems and literary writings of T'an. The author believes that they had two common features: liberation from convention and utilitarianism. Thus he rates T'an as a forerunner of the literary revolution of the May Fourth era.

193 **Yang I-feng** 楊一峯 , *T'an Ssu-t'ung* 譚嗣同 [T'an Ssu-t'ung]
Taipei: Chuan-chi ts'ung-shu, 1959. 130 pages

There are seven chapters, covering the life, the times, the thought, and the poems of T'an, with a conclusion on the various controversial issues. There is a chronological biography compiled by the author. In the bibliography, two important works published in mainland China have not been included—the *T'an Ssu-t'ung ch'üan-chi* and *T'an Ssu-t'ung nien-p'u*. The chronological biography, though slightly better than the one by Ch'en Nai-ch'ien, is hardly adequate for historians. Some of T'an's works, moreover, are misdated.

194 **Yang I-feng** 楊一峯 , "T'an Ssu-t'ung chih shih" 譚嗣同之詩 [The poems of T'an Ssu-t'ung]
In *Ch'ang-liu* 暢流 , Vol. 24, No. 11 (Jan. 1962), pp. 5-6.

The author analyses the poems of T'an and concludes that T'an's inclination to use Buddhist terms and neologisms means a liberation from convention and that T'an's poetry was generally good.

195 **Yang I-feng** 楊一峯 , "T'an Ssu-t'ung te Jen-hsüeh" 譚嗣同的仁學 [T'an Ssu-t'ung's *Jen-hsüeh*]

In *Min-chu hsien-cheng*民主憲政, Vol. 15, No. 1 (Nov. 1958), pp. 3-5; No. 2 (Nov. 1958), pp. 8-11.

196 **Yang I-feng** 楊一峯, **"T'an Ssu-t'ung te wen-hsüeh"** 譚嗣同的文學 [**The literary writings of T'an Ssu-t'ung**]
In *Min-chu hsien-cheng*民主憲政, Vol. 14, No. 6 (July 1958), pp. 9-11.

Discusses the literary style of T'an. Not much different from the above entry.

197 **Yang Jung-kuo** 楊榮國 *et al., Chien-ming Chung-kuo che-hsüeh shih* 簡明中國哲學史[**A concise history of Chinese philosophy**]
.Peking: Jen-min ch'u-pan-she, 1973, pp. 454-468.

Condensed mainly from his book *T'an Ssu-t'ung che-hsüeh ssu-hsiang.*

198 **Yang Jung-kuo** 楊榮國 *et al., Chien-ming Chung-kuo ssu-hsiang shih* 簡明中國思想史[**A concise history of Chinese thought**]
Peking: Chung-kuo ch'ing-nien ch'u-pan-she, 1962, pp. 228-231.

A brief introduction to T'an's thought. The author interprets T'an as a materialist.

199 **Yang Jung-kuo** 楊榮國 , *T'an Ssu-t'ung che-hsüeh ssu-hsiang* 譚嗣同哲學 思想 [**The philosophical thought of T'an Ssu-t'ung**]
Peking: Jen-min ch'u-pan-she, 1957. 52 pages.

The main philosophical inspirations for T'an, the author asserts, were the *"tao-ch'i"* ideas of Chang Tsai 張載 and the political thought of Huang Tsung-hsi 黃宗羲. *Jen* was pantheistic and pan-*jen*istic, and was therefore materialistic. Based on materialistic thinking, T'an criticized the blind adherence to names, and the stoic denial of human desires. His thought was historical, anti-religious, dialectical and scientific. He objected to feudalism in favour of capitalism. His political thinking was democratic and reformist
Criticized by Chu Jui-k'ai 祝瑞開.

200 **Yang Jung-kuo** 楊榮國, **"T'an Ssu-t'ung te Jen-hsüeh ssu-hsiang"** 譚嗣 同的仁學思想 [**The thought expressed in T'an Ssu-t'ung's** *Jen-hsüeh*]
In *Chung-hua lun-tan* 中華論壇 ,Vols. 5 and 6 (April 1945), pp. 20-27.

201 Yang T'ing-fu 楊廷福, "T'an Ssu-t'ung chu-tso shu-ch'i hsieh-tso nien-yüeh k'ao" 譚嗣同著作書啟寫作年月考 [Dating the works and letters of T'an Ssu-t'ung]

In *Fu-tan hsüeh-pao* 復旦學報, No. 1 (May 1956), pp. 177-193.

Also appeared in Chou K'ang-hsieh 周康燮 (ed.), *Chung-kuo chin-san-pai nien hsüeh-shu ssu-hsiang lun-chi erh-pien* 中國近三百年學術思想論集二編 [Second collection of articles on Chinese learning and thought of the last three hundred years]. Hong Kong: Ch'ung-wen shu-tien, 1971, pp. 225-241.

A detailed dating of the writings and letters of T'an Ssu-t'ung. Amazing, however, to find that some of this author's datings are widely at variance with those of Huang Chang-chien 黃彰健. Nonetheless, a useful guide to the loosely numbered and unchronologically arranged correspondence of T'an in *TSTCC*.

202 Yang T'ing-fu 楊廷福, *T'an Ssu-t'ung nien-p'u* 譚嗣同年譜 [A chronological biography of T'an Ssu-t'ung]

Peking: Jen-min ch'u-pan-she, 1957. 127 pages.

This chronological biography has several special features: (1) the provision of other pertinent data; (2) works dated according to both Chinese and Western calendars; (3) a Marxist orientation. Mistakes, however, are not lacking: (1) "Chih yen" 治言 is not, as the author thinks, progressive thinking but ethnocentric views; (2) this work was not written in 1885 but in 1889; (3) "Ssu-wei i-yün tai tuan-shu—pao Pei Yüan-cheng" 思緯壹壹臺短書——報貝元徵 is misdated 1894 when in fact it should be 1895; (4) T'an did not deliberately go to Peking to see K'ang Yu-wei in 1895 (this point made by Chang Te-chün 張德鈞); (5) the quotation on *tao-ch'i* ideas (p. 83) is not from the *Jen-hsüeh* but from the "Ssu-wei i-yün tai tuan-shu". Despite these mistakes, however, this work is up to now the most complete chronological biography of T'an.

203 Yen Ch'iu 燕丘, "T'an Ssu-t'ung che-hsüeh ssu-hsiang" 譚嗣同哲學思想 [The philosophical thought of T'an Ssu-t'ung]

In *Tu-shu yüeh-pao* 讀書月報, Vol. 5 (May 1957), p. 28.

A review of Yang Jung-kuo's book on T'an Ssu-t'ung. Criticizes Yang for his implausible explanation of T'an's idea of *jen*.

204 Yen Pei-ming 嚴北溟, "Lun T'an Ssu-t'ung te Jen-hsüeh ssu-hsiang"

論譚嗣同的仁學思想 **[On the thought of T'an Ssu-t'ung's *Jen-hsüeh*]**
In *Che-hsüeh yen-chiu* 哲學研究 , Vol. 2 (1962), pp. 41-53.

The author attacks the views of Fung Yu-lan, and believes that T'an's thought could only be idealistic. In comparing the relative importance of science and Buddhism, he thinks that the latter plays a more important role. The author also classifies materialistic interpretations of Ether under six heads: (1) Ether as the substance of *jen*; (2) Ether as molecular particles; (3) Ether as a materialistic concept; (4) Ether as mental power which has a materialistic nature; (5) Ether as a pantheistic substance; and (6) Ether as *chi* 氣 . The author attacks each in turn and concludes that Ether could only be idealistic and that this was because of T'an's interest in Buddhism.

205 **Yü Mu-jen** 余牧人, **"T'an Ssu-t'ung te tsung-chiao kuan"** 譚嗣同的宗教觀 **[The religious views of T'an Ssu-t'ung]**
In *Wen-she yüeh-k'an* 文社月刊 , Vol. 3, No. 4 (Feb. 1928), pp. 27-43; No. 5 (March 1928), pp. 11-31.

A substantial article dealing with T'an's religious views. Buddhism, the author says, was the religion most congenial to T'an. The author draws materials from the *Jen-hsüeh* and analyses them from several angles.

APPENDICES

A. A List of Chinese Publishers

Cheng-chung shu-chü (Taipei)	台北正中書局
Chin-ling yin-shu-kuan (Nanking)	南京金陵印書館
Chuan-chi ts'ung-shu (Taipei)	台北傳記叢書
Ch'ün-hsüeh she (Shanghai)	上海群學社
Chung-hua shu-chü (Peking)	北京中華書局
Chung-hua shu-chü (Shanghai)	上海中華書局
Chung-hua shu-chü (Taipei)	台北中華書局
Chung-hua wen-hua ch'u-pan shih-yeh she (Taipei)	台北中華文化出版事業社
Chung-hua wen-hua ch'u-pan shih-yeh wei-yüan-hui (Taipei)	台北中華文化出版事業委員會
Chung-kuo ch'ing-nien ch'u-pan-she (Peking)	北京中國青年出版社
Chung-yang yen-chiu-yüan li-shih yü-yen yen-chiu-so (Taipei)	台北中央研究院歷史語言研究所
Ch'ung-wen shu-tien (Hong Kong)	香港崇文書店
Hsiang-kang wen-hsüeh yen-chiu-she (Hong Kong)	香港　香港文學研究社
Hsin-chih-shih ch'u-pan-she (Shanghai)	上海新知識出版社
Hsin min she (Yokohama)	橫濱新民社
Hsüan-ho yin-she (Shanghai)	上海宣和印社
Hu-pei jen-min ch'u-pan-she (Wuhan)	武漢湖北人民出版社
Jen-min ch'u-pan-she (Peking)	北京人民出版社
Jen-min ch'u-pan-she (Shanghai)	上海人民出版社
Jen-min ch'u-pan-she (Shensi)	陝西人民出版社
Jen-wen yin-wu-she (Peking)	北京人文印務社
K'ai-ming shu-chü (Shanghai)	上海開明書局
K'o-hsüeh ch'u-pan-she (Peking)	北京科學出版社
Kuo-hsüeh fu-lun-she (Shanghai)	上海國學扶輪社
Kuo-min ch'u-pan-she (Taipei)	台北國民出版社
Kuo-min pao-she ch'u-yang hsüeh-sheng pien-i-so (Tokyo)	東京國民報社出洋學生編譯所
Lung-men shu-tien (Hong Kong)	香港龍門書店
San-lien shu-tien (Peking)	北京三聯書店
Shang-hai ch'u-pan kung-ssu (Shanghai)	上海　上海出版公司

Shang-wu yin-shu-kuan (Shanghai)	上海商務印書館
Shang-wu yin-shu-kuan (Taipei)	台北商務印書館
Shen-chou kuo-kuang-she (Shanghai)	上海神州國光社
Sheng-huo shu-tien (Shanghai)	上海生活書店
Shui-niu ch'u-pan-she (Taipei)	台北水牛出版社
Ta-chung shu-chü (Taipei)	台北大中書局
Ta-t'ung shu-chü (Taipei)	台北大同書局
Tung-ta t'u-shu yu-hsien kung-ssu (Taipei)	台北東大圖書有限公司
Wen-hai ch'u-pan-she (Taipei)	台北文海出版社
Wen-hua kung-ying-she (Shanghai)	上海文化供應社
Wen-i shu-wu (Hong Kong)	香港文藝書屋
Wen-hsing shu-tien (Taipei)	台北文星書店
Wen-ming ch'u-pan-she (Shanghai)	上海文明出版社
Yen-ching ta-hsüeh kuo-hsüeh yen-chiu-so (Peking)	北京燕京大學國學研究所
Yu-shih wen-hua shih-yeh kung-ssu (Taipei)	台北幼獅文化事業公司
Yüan-tung t'u-shu kung-ssu (Hong Kong)	香港遠東圖書公司

B. A List of Periodicals and Newspapers

Ch'ang-liu (February 1950–)　　　　　　暢流
　　Taipei: Ch'ang-liu pan-yüeh-k'an she　　台北：暢流半月刊社
Che-hsüeh yen-chiu (1955–)　　　　　　哲學研究
　　Peking: Che-hsüeh yen-chiu tsa-chih she　北京：哲學研究雜誌社
Cheng-chih p'ing-lun (September 1958–)　政治評論
　　Taipei: Cheng-chih p'ing-lun pien-chi　台北：政治評論編輯委員會
　　wei-yüan-hui
Chiang-han hsüeh-pao (1961–)　　　　　江漢學報
　　Wuchang: Chiang-han hsüeh-pao she　　武昌：江漢學報社
Chiao-hsüeh yü yen-chiu (1957–)　　　　教學與研究
　　Peking: Chung-kuo jen-min ta-hsüeh　　北京：中國人民大學
Ch'ing-ho (November 1932–August 1937)　青鶴
　　Shanghai: Ch'ing-ho tsa-chih she　　　上海：青鶴雜誌社
Ch'ing-hua hsüeh-pao (June 1924–)　　　清華學報
　　Peking: Ch'ing-hua ta-hsüeh　　　　　北京：清華大學
Ch'ing-i pao (1898–1901)　　　　　　　清議報
　　Yokohama: Hsin-min she　　　　　　橫濱：新民社
Chuan-chi wen-hsüeh (1962–)　　　　　傳記文學
　　Taipei: Chuan-chi wen-hsüeh pien-chi-　台北：傳記文學編輯委員會
　　wei-yüan-hui
Ch'un-ch'iu (June 1964–)　　　　　　春秋
　　Taipei: Ch'un-ch'iu tsa-chih pien-chi-　台北：春秋雜誌編輯委員會
　　wei-yüan-hui
Chung-hua jih-pao (1947–)　　　　　　中華日報
　　Taipei: Chung-kuo kuo-min-tang tang-　台北：中國國民黨黨營文化事
　　ying wen-hua shih-yeh chuan-chi pien-　業專輯編纂委員會
　　tsuan wei-yüan-hui
Chung-hua lun-tan (February 1945–　　　中華論壇
　　December 1946)　　　　　　　　　上海：中華論壇社
　　Shanghai: Chung-hua lun-tan she
Chung-kuo chien-she (October 1945–　　　中國建設
　　April 1949)　　　　　　　　　　上海：中國建設出版社
　　Shanghai: Chung-kuo chien-she ch'u-
　　pan-she

69

Chung-wai tsa-chih (March 1967–)　　　　中外雜誌
　　Taipei: Chung-wai tsa-chih she　　　　台北：中外雜誌社
Chung-yang jih-pao (12th March, 1949–)　中央日報
　　Taipei: Chung-yang jih-pao she　　　　台北：中央日報社
Chung-yang ta-hsüeh pan-yüeh-k'an　　　中央大學半月刊
　　(October 1929–January 1931)　　　　南京：中央大學
　　Nanking: Chung-yang ta-hsüeh
Fu-tan hsüeh-pao (1956–)　　　　　　　復旦學報
　　Shanghai: Fu-tan ta-hsüeh　　　　　　上海：復旦大學
Hsiang-pao (March 1898–October 1898)　　湘報
　　Hunan: Hsiang-pao she　　　　　　　　湖南：湘報社
Hsien-tai tsa-chih (1965–)　　　　　　現代雜誌
　　Hong Kong: Hsien-tai tsa-chih she　　香港：現代雜誌社
Hsin chien-she (1949–)　　　　　　　　新建設
　　Peking: Kuang-ming jih-pao she　　　北京：光明日報社
Hsin hsia (1969–)　　　　　　　　　　新夏
　　Taipei: Hsin-hsia yüeh-k'an she　　台北：新夏月刊社
Hsin-min tsung-pao (1902–1907)　　　　新民叢報
　　Yokohama: Hsin-min tsung-pao she　　橫濱：新民叢報社
Hsin shih-hsüeh t'ung-hsün (1951–1956)　新史學通訊
　　K'aifeng, Honan　　　　　　　　　　開封、河南
Hsin shih-tai (1961–)　　　　　　　　新時代
　　Taipei: Hsin shih-tai tsa-chih she　台北：新時代雜誌社
Hsin-ya hsüeh-sheng pao (1966–)　　　新亞學生報
　　Hong Kong: Hsin-ya hsüeh-sheng-hui　香港：新亞學生會
Hsing shih (1925–)　　　　　　　　　醒獅
　　Taipei: Hsing-shih tsa-chih she　　台北：醒獅雜誌社
Hsüeh-shu yüeh-k'an (1958–)　　　　　學術月刊
　　Shanghai: Hsüeh-shu yüeh-k'an pien-　上海：學術月刊編委會
　　wei-hui
Hu-nan li-shih tzu-liao (1958–1961)　　湖南歷史資料
　　Changsha: Hu-nan jen-min ch'u-pan-she　長沙：湖南人民出版社
Hu-nan wen-hsien (1972–)　　　　　　湖南文獻
　　Taipei: Hu-nan wen-hsien she　　　　台北：湖南文獻社
Hua-ch'iao jih-pao (1945–)　　　　　華僑日報
　　Hong Kong: Hua-ch'iao jih-pao yu-hsien　香港：華僑日報有限公司
　　kung-ssu

70

I wen chih (October 1965–)　　　　　　藝文誌
　　Taipei: I-wen-chih wen-hua shih-yeh　台北：藝文誌文化事業有限公司
　　yu-hsien kung-ssu
Jen-min jih-pao (1946–)　　　　　　　人民日報
　　Peking: Jen-min jih-pao she　　　　北京：人民日報社
Jen-wen tsa-chih (1930–)　　　　　　人文雜誌
　　Shanghai: Jen-wen pien-chi-so　　　上海：人文編輯所
Kuang-ming jih-pao (1950–)　　　　　光明日報
　　Peking: Kuang-ming jih-pao she　　北京：光明日報社
Kuei-chou jih-pao　　　　　　　　　貴州日報
　　Kueichou: Kuei-chou jih-pao she　　貴州：貴州日報社
Kung-pao yüeh-k'an　　　　　　　　公報月刊
　　Taipei: Kung-pao yüeh-k'an pien-chi　台北：公報月刊編輯委員會
　　wei-yüan-hui
Li-lun yü hsien-shih (April 1939–March　理論與現實
　　1947)　　　　　　　　　　　　重慶：生活書店
　　Chungking: Sheng-huo shu-tien
Li-shih yen chiu (February 1954–)　　歷史研究
　　Peking: Li-shih yen-chiu tsa-chih she　北京：歷史研究雜誌社
Min-chu hsien-cheng (March 1951–)　民主憲政
　　Taipei: Min-chu hsien-cheng pien-chi　台北：民主憲政編輯委員會
　　wei-yüan-hui
Min-ch'üan su (April 1914 –April 1916)　民權素
　　Shanghai: Min-ch'üan ch'u-pan-pu　上海：民權出版部
Pao-hsüeh chi-k'an (October 1934 –August　報學季刊
　　1935)　　　　　　　　　　　　上海：電時電訊社
　　Shanghai: Tien-shih tien-hsün she
Pei-ching jih-pao (1955–)　　　　　北京日報
　　Peking: Pei-ching jih-pao she　　　北京：北京日報社
Pei-ching ta-hsüeh hsüeh-pao (1957–)　北京大學學報
　　Peking: Pei-ching ta-hsüeh　　　　北京：北京大學
Sheng-li yüeh-k'an (1967–)　　　　生力月刊
　　Taipei: Sheng-li yüeh-k'an-she　　台北：生力月刊社
Shih-hsüeh hui-k'an (1959–)　　　　史學會刊
　　Taipei: Tai-wan shih-fan ta-hsüeh li-shih　台北：台灣師範大學歷史學會
　　hsüeh-hui
Shih-wu pao (August 1896–July 1898)　時務報
　　Shanghai: Shih-wu pao kuan　　　上海：時務報館

Shih yüan (July 1970–)　　　　　　　　　　史原
　　Taipei: Tai-wan ta-hsüeh li-shih-hsüeh　　台北：台灣大學歷史學研究所
　　yen-chiu-so

Ta-lu tsa-chih (1950–)　　　　　　　　　　大陸雜誌
　　Taipei: Ta-lu tsa-chih she　　　　　　　　台北：大陸雜誌社

T'ien-wen-tai (1936–)　　　　　　　　　　天文台
　　Hong Kong: T'ien-wen-t'ai ch'u-pan-she　　香港：天文台出版社

Tsai-sheng (April 1932–)　　　　　　　　　再生
　　Taipei: Tsai-sheng tsa-chih she　　　　　　台北：再生雜誌社

Tu-shu yüeh-pao (1955–)　　　　　　　　　讀書月報
　　Peking: Tu-shu yüeh-pao she　　　　　　　北京：讀書月報社

Tung-fang tsa-chih (July 1967–)　　　　　　東方雜誌
　　Taipei: Tung-fang tsa-chih she　　　　　　台北：東方雜誌社

Tung-nan hua-pao (1957–)　　　　　　　　東南畫報
　　Taipei: Tung-nan hua-pao chou-k'an she　　台北：東南畫報週刊社

Tzu-li wan-pao (1961–)　　　　　　　　　　自立晚報
　　Taipei: Tzu-li wan-pao she　　　　　　　　台北：自立晚報社

Wen-hua chien-she (October 1934–July　　　文化建設
　　1937)　　　　　　　　　　　　　　　　上海：文化建設月刊
　　Shanghai: Wen-hua chien-she yüeh-k'an

Wen-hua p'i-p'an (May 1934–January　　　　文化批判
　　1941)　　　　　　　　　　　　　　　　重慶：文化批判社
　　Chungking: Wen-hua p'i-p'an she

Wen-hsüeh i-ch'an tseng-k'an (1955–)　　　文學遺產增刊
　　Peking: Tso-chia ch'u-pan-she　　　　　　北京：作家出版社

Wen-she yüeh-k'an (October 1925–1926?)　　文社月刊
　　Suchou: Tung-wu ta-hsüeh Chung-hua　　蘇州：東吳大學中華基督教文社
　　Chi-tu-chiao wen-she

Wen-shih (October 1962–)　　　　　　　　文史
　　Peking: Chung-hua shu-chü　　　　　　　北京：中華書局

Wen shih che (May 1951–)　　　　　　　　文史哲
　　Chinan: Shan-tung ta-hsüeh wen-shih　　濟南：山東大學文史雜誌社
　　tsa-chih she

Yü-wen chiao-hsüeh (August 1951–)　　　　語文教學
　　Peking: Yü-wen chiao-hsüeh she　　　　　北京：語文教學社

Yü-wen hsüeh-hsi (October 1951–)　　　　語文學習
　　Peking: K'ai-ming shu-tien　　　　　　　北京：開明書店

C. Title Index

The Buddhist Theme in Late Ch'ing Political Thought: 1890-1911, with Special Reference to T'an Ssu-t'ung, 001

D. Author Index in Chronological Order

Author Index in Chronological Order

E. Subject Index

F. A Chronology of the Writings of T'an Ssu-t'ung

Between 1958 and 1960, the *Historical Materials on Hunan* (Hu-nan li-shih tzu-liao 湖南歷史資料) published a wealth of information about T'an Ssu-t'ung which had not been collected in *The Complete Works of T'an Ssu-t'ung* (T'an Ssu-t'ung ch'üan-chi 譚嗣同全集). However, most of the materials in these two sources are undated and misleadingly numbered. For the last fifteen years, historians such as Huang Chang-chien 黃彰健 and Yang T'ing-fu 楊廷福 have made enormous effort to date them. But their findings are often widely at variance. This is caused partly by the lack of concrete facts in some of T'an's writings which would enable a correct dating, but above all, by the unavailability of the *Hunan Daily* (Hsiang-pao 湘報) in which most of T'an's political essays were published. Recently, I was able to consult the complete set of the newspaper which gave me an enormous advantage in dating some of T'an's more important essays. Chronologies like this can never be perfect. But if the more important writings have been properly dated, then it seems to me that the purpose of compiling this chronology is already served.

ABBREVIATIONS:

CC for *T'an Ssu-t'ung ch'üan-chi* 譚嗣同全集 .
HN for *Hu-nan li-shih tzu-liao* 湖南歷史資料 .
In the citation of dates, (KH20, 5.21), for example, means the twenty-first of the fifth month of the twentieth year of Kuang-hsü's reign.

NOTES:

(1) Unless stated otherwise, the titles refer to poems that T'an wrote.
(2) T'an's age is calculated according to the Chinese lunar calendar.
(3) Any undated work placed in between two specific dates means that the work was probably written sometime during the interval.

REFERENCES:

Ch'en Nai-ch'ien 陳乃乾 , "Liu-yang T'an hsien-sheng nien-p'u" 瀏陽譚先生年譜 [A chronological biography of Mr. T'an Ssu-t'ung of Liuyang]. In *T'an Liu-yang ch'üan-chi* 譚瀏陽全集 [Collected works of T'an Ssu-t'ung of Liuyang]. Shanghai: Shang-hai wen-ming ch'u-pan-she, 1952, pp. 11-27.
Hu-nan li-shih tzu-liao 湖南歷史資料 [Historical materials on Hunan], Vol. 3 (1958) to Vol. 9 (1960).

Huang Chang-chien 黃彰健, "T'an Ssu-t'ung ch'üan-chi shu-cha hsi-nien" 譚嗣同全集書扎繫年 [Dating T'an's letters in the *Complete Works of T'an Ssu-t'ung*]. In Huang Chang-chien, *Wu-hsü pien-fa shih yen-chiu* 戊戌變法史研究 [Studies on the 1898 Reform Movement]. Taipei: Chung-yang yen-chiu-yüan li-shih yü-yen yen-chiu-so, 1970, pp. 627-660.

Jung Meng-yüan 榮孟源, *Chung-kuo chin-tai shih li piao* 中國近代史曆表 [Chronological tables for the years 1830-1949]. Peking: San-lien shu-tien, 1953.

Liang Ch'i-ch'ao 梁啓超, "T'an Ssu-t'ung chuan" 譚嗣同傳 [A biography of T'an Ssu-t'ung]. In *Ch'ing-i pao* 清議報, Vol. 4 (22nd January, 1899), pp. 4-7.

T'an Ssu-t'ung 譚嗣同, *T'an Ssu-t'ung ch'üan-chi* 譚嗣同全集 [Complete works of T'an Ssu-t'ung]. Peking: San-lien shu-tien, 1954.

Yang T'ing-fu 楊廷福, "T'an Ssu-t'ung chu-tso shu-ch'i hsieh-tso nien-yüeh k'ao" 譚嗣同著作書啓寫作年月考 [Dating the works and letters of T'an Ssu-t'ung]. In *Fu-tan hsüeh-pao* 復旦學報, No. 1 (May 1956), pp. 177-193.

Yang T'ing-fu 楊廷福, *T'an Ssu-t'ung nien-p'u* 譚嗣同年譜 [A chronological biography of T'an Ssu-t'ung]. Peking: Jen-min ch'u-pan-she, 1957.

1877 (Kuang-hsü 3rd year. Ting-ch'ou 丁丑 . Age: 13)

December
(KH2, 11)
Shang ta po-fu-mu shu erh 上大伯父母書二 [Letter to my father's eldest brother and his wife, No. 2]
— HN: Vol. 5, p. 78.

1879 (Kuang-hsü 5th year. Chi-mao 己卯 . Age: 15)

Autumn
Sung-pieh chung-hsiung Ssu-sheng fu Ch'in Lung sheng-fu 送別仲兄泗生赴秦隴省父 [Bidding farewell to my elder brother Ssu-hsiang 嗣襄 who went to Ch'in-chou in Kansu to visit our father]
— CC: p. 487.

1882 (Kuang-hsü 8th year. Jen-wu 壬午 . Age: 18)

June
(KH8, 5)
Shang ta po-fu-mu shu i 上大伯父母書一 [Letter to my father's eldest brother and his wife, No. 1]
— HN: Vol. 5, p. 77.

Autumn
Shang ta po-fu-mu shu ssu 上大伯父母書四 [Letter to my father's eldest brother and his wife, No. 4]
— HN: Vol. 5, pp. 78-79.

November
(10)
Shang ta po-fu-mu shu san 上大伯父母書三 [Letter to my father's eldest brother and his wife, No. 3]
— HN: Vol. 5, p. 78.
Hsüeh yeh 雪夜 [Snowy night]
— CC: p. 465.
Lan-chou Chuang-yen ssu 蘭州莊嚴寺 [The Chuang-yen Temple in Lan-chou in Kansu]
— CC: p. 465.
T'ung-kuan 潼關 [The T'ung Pass]
— CC: p. 489.
Tao-chia erh p'ien 到家二篇 [On arriving home]
— CC: p. 492.
Yu Ch'in Lung fu Kan Lan tao chung chi-shih 由秦隴赴甘蘭道中即事 [An extempore poem composed while travelling from Ch'in-chou to Lan-chou and Kan-chou in Kansu]
— CC: p. 493.

1883 (Kuang-hsü 9th year. Kuei-wei 癸未 . Age: 19)

Su t'ien-chia 宿田家 [Lodging at a farmhouse]
— CC: p. 451.

Lung shan 隴山 [Mountain Lung in Shensi]
— CC: p. 462.

Ping ch'i 病起 [Recovering from an illness]
— CC: p. 465.

Ch'iu-jih chiao-wai 秋日郊外 [Countryside on an autumn day]
— CC: p. 466.

Tung yeh 冬夜 [Winter night]
— CC: p. 466.

Lan-chou Wang-shih yüan-lin 蘭州王氏園林 [Wang's family garden in Lan-chou, Kansu]
— CC: p. 471.

Pai ts'ao-yüan 白草原 [A white grassland]
— CC: p. 471.

Ku i 古意 [Nostalgia]
— CC: p. 492.

1884 (Kuang-hsü 10th year. Chia-shen 甲申 . Age: 20)

Ho liang yin 河梁吟 [Parting at a bridge]
— CC: p. 451.

Pieh i 別意 [Feelings at parting]
— CC: p. 452.

Hsi-yü yin 西域引 [A song of the western territories]
— CC: p. 457.

Tao Wu shan 道吾山 [Mount Tao Wu in Liuyang, Hunan]
— CC: p. 466.

Chüeh sheng 角聲 [Horn blare]
— CC: p. 467.

Ma shang tso 馬上作 [Composed on horse back]
— CC: p. 468.

1885 (Kuang-hsü 11th year. Chi-yu 己酉 . Age: 21)

Chiang hsing 江行 [Sailing on a river]
— CC: p. 467.

Yeh po 夜泊 [Mooring at night]
— CC: p. 467.

Pieh Lan-chou 別蘭州 [Leaving Lan-chou, Kansu]
— CC: p. 467.

Lao ma 老馬 [Old horse]
— CC: p. 468.

Tung-t'ing yeh po 洞庭夜泊 [Night mooring at Lake Tung-t'ing]
— CC: p. 468.

Teng-shan kuan yü 登山觀雨 [Climbing up a mountain to watch rain]
— CC: p. 479.

Ch'u-hsi Shang-chou chi chung-hsiung 除夕商州寄仲兄 [A poem sent to my elder brother from Shang-chou, Kansu, on New Year's Eve]
— CC: p. 494.

1887 (Kuang-hsü 13th year. Ting-hai 丁亥. Age: 23)

T'ui yüan 蛻園 [Garden Exuviae]
— CC: p. 457.

Ts'an-hun ch'ü 殘魂曲 [A song of my remaining years]
— CC: p. 457.

Ch'i-yüan yü san p'ien 憩園雨三篇 [Three stanzas on rain at Garden Rest]
— CC: p. 473.

Tseng ju-sai jen 贈入塞人 [To a friend heading for the frontier]
— CC: p. 480.

Ho Ching Ch'iu-p'ing shih-lang Kan-su tsung-tu-shu Fu-yün-lou shih erh p'ien 和景秋平侍郎甘肅總督拂雲樓詩二篇 [Responding to Vice-minister Ching Ch'iu-p'ing's poem on the Fu-yün Tower in the Kansu Governor's official lodging, using the same rhymes]
— CC: p. 480.

1888 (Kuang-hsü 14the year. Wu-tzu 戊子. Age: 24)

Ch'in-ling 秦嶺 [Ch'inling in Shensi]
— CC: p. 457.

Erh lan ch'uan ping hsü 兒纜船丼紋 [A child pulling a boat, with preface]
— CC: p. 461.

San yüan-yang p'ien 三鴛鴦篇 [Three mandarin ducks]
— CC: p. 461.

Ying-su mi-nang yao 罌粟米囊謠 [A song of poppy and rice-bag]
— CC: p. 462.

Liu-p'an-shan chuan-hsiang yao 六盤山轉饟謠 [A song of transporting rice at Mount Liu-p'an, Kansu]
— CC: p. 463.

Sui i 隨意 [An occasional poem]
— CC: p. 469.

Su Han 泝漢 [Up the River Han]
— CC: p. 469.

Sung Hui-tsung hua ying erh p'ien 宋徽宗畫鷹二篇 [Two stanzas on an eagle painting by Emperor Hui of Sung]
— CC: p. 489.

K'u Wu-ling Ch'en Hsing-wu Huan-k'uei san p'ien 哭武陵陳星五煥奎三篇 [Mourning the late Ch'en Hsing-wu of Wu-ling, Hunan]
— CC: p. 494.

1889 (Kuang-hsü 15th year. Chi-ch'ou 己丑 . Age: 25)

Chih yen 治言 [A treatise on politics]
— CC: pp. 103-109.

Chi chung-hsiung T'ai-wan 寄仲兄臺灣 [To my elder brother in Taiwan]
— CC: p. 469.

Ch'u T'ung-kuan tu-ho 出潼關渡河 [Crossing the Yellow River outside the T'ung Pass]
— CC: p. 469

Te chung-hsiung T'ai-wan shu kan-fu erh p'ien 得仲兄臺灣書感賦二篇 [On receiving a letter from my elder brother in Taiwan]
— CC: p. 473.

Lu-kou ch'iao 盧溝橋 [Bridge Lu-kou]
— CC: p. 470.

Ching-hsing kuan 井陘關 [The Ching-hsing Pass]
— CC: p. 490.

Li-shan wen-ch'üan 驪山溫泉 [A hotspring at Mount Li]
— CC: p. 490.

Ch'in-ling Han Wen-kung ts'u 秦嶺韓文公祠 [The Han Yü 韓愈 shrine at Ch'inling, Shensi]
— CC: p. 490.

Wu kuan 武關 [The Wu Pass]
— CC: p. 493.

Lan ch'iao 藍橋 [The Lan Bridge]
— CC: p. 493.

Hsien ts'ung-hsiung Fu-feng i-hsiang tsan ping hsü 先從兄馥
峯遺像贊並敍 [A eulogy on a portrait of my late first
cousin, Ssu-fen 嗣棻, with preface]
— CC: p. 508.

K'ung-t'ung 崆峒 [Mount K'ung-t'ung]
— CC: p. 480.

Tzu P'ing-liang Liu-hu chih Ching-chou tao chung 自平涼柳
湖至涇州道中 [Journey from Lake Liu of P'ing-liang to
Ching-chou, Kansu]
— CC: p. 480.

1890 (Kuang-hsü 16th year. Keng-yin 庚寅. Age: 26)

Before May
(KH16, 4)
Shang Ou-yang Pan-chiang shih shu shih-ch'i 上歐陽瓣薑師
書十七 [Letter to my teacher Ou-yang Chung-ku 歐陽中鵠,
No. 17]
— CC: pp. 313-314.

April-May
(3-4)
Hsiang-hen tz'u pa p'ien ping hsü 湘痕詞八篇並敍 [Recol-
lections of Hunan, a tz'u with preface]
— CC: pp. 452-454.

April
(3)
Wen Hsin-kuo jih-yüeh hsing-ch'en yen ko ping hsü 文信國日
月星辰硯歌幷敍 [The "Jih-yüeh hsing-ch'en" inkstone of
Wen T'ien-hsiang, a song with preface]
— CC: p. 464.

April
(3)
Wen Hsin-kuo kung Chiao-yü ch'in chi 文信國公蕉雨琴記 [An
account of the revered Wen T'ien-hsiang's Chiao-yü lute]
— See Chou K'ang-hsieh.

Kung yen 公讌 [A public banquet]
— CC: p. 455.

Pi t'ien tung 碧天洞 [The Pi-t'ien Cave]
— CC: p. 456.

Ku pieh-li 古別離 [The Sadness of departing]
— CC: p. 463.

T'ao-hua fu-jen miao shen-hsien ch'ü san p'ien 桃花夫人廟神
絃曲三篇 [Three hymns for Madame Ch'u Hsi 楚息夫人
Temple]
— CC: p. 459.

Wu-ch'ang yeh po 武昌夜泊 [Night mooring at Wuchang]
— CC: p. 470.

An-ch'ing Tai-kuan-t'ing 安慶大觀亭 [The Tai-kuan Pavilion in Anching, Anhui]
— CC: p. 481.

Ts'an hsieh 殘蟹 [Crippled crab]
— CC: p. 481.

Chi Hung-shan hsing-shih 記洪山形勢 [On the topography of Mount Hung]
— CC: p. 169.

1891 (Kuang-hsü 17th year Hsin-mao 辛卯 . Age: 27)

Liu Yün-t'ien chuan 劉雲田傳 [A biography of Liu Yün-t'ien]
— CC: pp. 170-172.

Tai ta-jen chuan tseng feng-cheng ta-fu Jen chün mu-chih-ming ping hsü 代大人撰贈奉政大夫任君墓志銘並敍 [Composing for my father the epitaph of the honourable Mr. Jen (Pen-yao 任本堯), with preface]
— CC: p. 497.

Chi tu ko ping hsü 極蠹歌並敍 [A song about corruption, with preface]
— CC: p. 455.

Hu-pei hsün-fu-shu Liu-hsü-t'ing wan-t'iao t'ung Jao Hsien-ch'a tso 湖北巡撫署六虛亭晚眺同饒仙槎作 [A poem written to Jao Hsien-ch'a when watching sunset from the Liu-hsü Pavilion in the Hupei Governor's official lodging]
— CC: p. 456.

Hsiao Hsiang wan-ching t'u erh p'ien 瀟湘晚景圖二篇 [An evening scene by the rivers Hsiao and Hsiang]
— CC: p. 489.

Lun i chüeh-chü liu p'ien 論藝絕句六篇 [On art]
— CC: p. 490.

Wu-ch'ang t'a-ch'ing tz'u 武昌踏青詞 [Spring outing in Wu-chang]
— CC: p. 482.

December
(KH17, 11)
Yüan-i-t'ang chi wai wen ch'u-p'ien tzu-hsü 遠遺堂集外文初編自敍 [Editor's preface to the first supplement to (my elder brother's) *Collected Works of the Yüan-i Studio*]
— CC: p. 151.

1893 (Kuang-hsü 19th year. Kuei-ssu 癸巳. Age: 29)

February-March
(KH19, 1-2)

Yüan-i-t'ang chi wai wen hsü-p'ien tzu-hsü 遠遺堂集外文續編自敘 [Editor's preface to the second supplement to (my elder brother's) *Collected Works of the Yüan-i Studio*]
— CC: p. 152.

San-jen hsiang-tsan ping hsü 三人像贊并敘 [A eulogy on a photograph of three of us (T'an Ssu-t'ung, Jao Hsien-ch'a 饒仙槎 and Li Cheng-tse 李正則), with preface]
— CC: p. 507.

Teng chen-nü shih ping chuang 鄧貞女詩并狀 [A biographical sketch of the virtuous lady Teng (Lien-ku 聯姑)]
— CC: pp. 459-460.

Ch'eng-nan ssu-chiu ming ping hsü 城南思舊銘并敘 [Recollections of the southern part of the town, with preface]
— CC: pp. 499-500.

Ho Hsien-ch'a ch'u-hsi kan-huai ssu p'ien ping hsü 和仙槎除夕感懷四篇并敘 [Responding to (Jao) Hsien-ch'a's poem "Thoughts on New Year's Eve", using the same rhymes, with preface]
— CC: p. 482.

Autumn

Yü Shen Hsiao-i shu i 與沈小沂書一 [Letter to Shen Hsiao-i, No. 1]
— CC: pp. 430-431.

26 November
(10.19)

Shang Ou-yang Pan-chiang shih shu ch'i 上歐陽瓣薑師書七 [Letter to my teacher Ou-yang Chung-ku, No. 7]
— CC: p. 305.

1894 (Kuang-hsü 20th year. Chia-wu 甲午. Age: 30)

Shih-chü-ying lu pi-chih 石菊影廬筆識 [Notes from the Shih-chü-ying Studio]
— CC: pp. 213-279.

Spring

Yü Shen Hsiao-i shu erh 與沈小沂書二 [Letter to Shen Hsiao-i, No. 2]
— CC: pp. 432-435.

Spring

Chih Lung Yü-ch'i shu i 致龍莪溪書一 [Letter to Lung Fu-jui 紱瑞, No. 1]
— CC: pp. 435-436.

Spring

Chih Liu Sung-fu shu san 致劉淞芙書三 [Letter to Liu Shan-han 劉善涵, No. 3]
— CC: pp. 381-382.

97

Chih Liu Sung-fu shu wu 致劉淞芙書五 [Letter to Liu Shan-han, No. 5]
　　— CC: pp. 383-384.

Chih Liu Sung-fu shu ch'i 致劉淞芙書七 [Letter to Liu Shan-han, No. 7]
　　— CC: pp. 385-386.

Pao Pei Yüan-cheng shu 報貝元徵書 [A letter in reply to Pei Yün-hsi 貝允昕]
　　— CC: pp. 386-389.

Hsien chung-hsiung hsing-shu 先仲兄行述 [Accounts of my late elder brother]
　　— CC: pp. 200-204.

Hsien-pi Hsü fu-jen i-shih chuang 先妣徐夫人逸事狀 [Anecdotes of my late mother, Nee Hsü (Wu-yüan 五緣)]
　　— CC: pp. 197-200.

Shih li tzu-hsü 史例自敍 [Preface to the format of a history book]
　　— CC: p. 154.

Chung-shu Ssu-shu i tzu-hsü 仲叔四書義自敍 [Author's preface to the commentaries on the *Four Books* by my elder brother Ssu-hsiang 嗣襄 and Ssu-t'ung]
　　— CC: pp. 155-157.

November-December (11)	Liu-yang T'an shih p'u hsü-li 瀏陽譚氏譜敍例 [Introductory remarks to the *Genealogy of the T'an Clan of Liu-yang, Hunan*] 　　— CC: pp. 157-167.
November-December (11)	Ch'i-huan fu-chün chia-chuan 啓寰府君家傳 [A family biography of my ancestor T'an Ch'i-huan] 　　— CC: pp. 172-173.
November-December (11)	Ch'ung-an hou Chuang-chieh kung chia-chuan 崇安侯壯節公家傳 [A family biography of T'an Yüan 譚淵 , Marquis of Chung-an] 　　— CC: pp. 173-176.
November-December	Hsin-ning po Chin-ch'en kung chia-chuan 新甯伯藎臣公家傳 [A family biography of T'an Chung 譚忠 , Count of Hsin-ning] 　　— CC: pp. 173-176.
December 1894- January 1895 (12)	T'ai-fu Hsin-ning po Chuang-hsi kung chia-chuan 太傅新甯伯莊僖公家傳 [A family biography of Imperial Tutor T'an Yin-yu 譚蔭祐 , Count of Hsin-ning] 　　— CC: pp. 179-180.

98

Hsin-ning po P'ing-man kung chia-chuan 新甯伯平蠻公家傳 [A family biography of T'an Tsung-lun 譚宗綸 , Count of Hsin-ning]
    — CC: pp. 180-181.
I-ts'ai fu-chün chia-chuan 逸才府君家傳 [A family biography of my ancestor T'an Kuo-piao 譚國表]
    — CC: pp. 181-183.
Chün-hsüan fu-chün chia-chuan 濬軒府君家傳 [A family biography of my ancestor T'an Shih-ch'ang 譚世昌]
    — CC: pp. 183-187.
Hsi-t'ing fu-chün chia-chuan 熙亭府君家傳 [A family biography of my ancestor T'an Wen-ming 譚文明]
    — CC: pp. 187-188.
Pu-hsiang fu-chün chia-chuan 步襄府君家傳 [A family biography of my ancestor T'an Hsüeh-ch'in 譚學琴]
    — CC: pp. 188-190.
Shao-ssu fu-chün chia-chuan 紹泗府君家傳 [A family biography of my ancestor T'an Hsüeh-hsin 譚學新]
    — CC: pp. 190-192.
Hai-chiao fu-chün chia-chuan 海嶠府君家傳 [A family biography of my ancestor T'an Chi-sheng 譚繼昇]
    — CC: pp. 192-193.
Chung-i chia-chuan 忠義家傳 [Family biographies of my ancestors known for loyalty and righteousness]
    — CC: pp. 193-195.
Chieh-hsiao chia-chuan 節孝家傳 [Family biographies of my ancestors' wives known for virtue and filial piety]
    — CC: pp. 195-197.

Winter   Ch'iu-yü nien-hua chih kuan ts'ung-ts'uo shu hsü 秋雨年華之館叢脞書敍 [Preface to the *Miscellaneous Writings from the Ch'iu-yü nien-hua Studio*]

Winter   — CC: p. 154.
Mang-ts'ang-ts'ang chai shih tzu-hsü 莽蒼蒼齋詩自敍 [Author's preface to the *Collected Poems from the Mang-ts'ang-ts'ang Studio*]
    — CC: p. 154.
Chih Liu Sung-fu shu i 致劉淞芙書一 [Letter to Liu Shan-han, No. 1]
    — CC: pp. 375-377.
Chih Liu Sung-fu shu erh 致劉淞芙書二 [Letter to Liu

99

Shan-han, No. 2]
— CC: pp. 378-381.

1895 (Kuang-hsü 21st year. I-wei 乙未. Age: 31)

12 January
(KH20, 12.17)
Chih Liu Sung-fu shu ssu 致劉淞芙書四 [Letter to Liu Shan-han, No. 4]
— CC: pp. 382-383.

January
(KH20, 12)
San-shih tzu-chi 三十自紀 [Autobiography at thirty]
— CC: pp. 204-207.

21 January
(KH20, 12.26)
Shang Ou-yang Pan-chiang shih shu i 上歐陽瓣薑師書一 [Letter to my teacher Ou-yang Chung-ku, No. 1]
— CC: pp. 285-287.

20 February
(KH21, 1.26)
Chih Chi Yün shu 致薊雲書 [A letter to Chi Yün]
— HN: Vol. 3, pp. 77-78.

March
Chih Liu Sung-fu shu i 致劉淞芙書一 [Letter to Liu Shan-han, No. 1]
— HN: Vol. 4, pp. 58-59.

April
(3)
Chih Liu Sung-fu shu ssu 致劉淞芙書四 [Letter to Liu Shan-han, No. 4]
— HN: Vol. 4, pp. 60-61.

April
(3)
Chih Liu Sung-fu shu san 致劉淞芙書三 [Letter to Liu Shan-han, No. 3]
— HN: Vol. 4, p. 60.

Chih Liu Sung-fu shu wu 致劉淞芙書五 [Letter to Liu Shan-han, No. 5]
— HN: Vol. 4, pp. 61-63.

May
(5)
I-wei tai Lung Chih-sheng shih-lang tsou-ch'ing pien-t'ung k'o-chü hsien ts'ung sui-k'o-shih ch'i che 乙未代龍芝生侍郎奏請變通科舉先從歲科試起折 [A memorial written in 1895 for Vice-minister Lung Chan-lin 龍湛霖 recommending a change in the civil examinations beginning with the annual candidacy examination]
— HN: Vol. 8, pp. 113-115.

June
(5)
Shang Ou-yang Pan-chiang shih shu erh—hsing suan-hsüeh i 上歐陽瓣薑師書二—興算學議 [Letter to my teacher Ou-yang Chung-ku, No. 2—a proposal to promote the study of mathematics]
— CC: pp. 187-202.

16 August
(6.26)
Shang Ou-yang Pan-chiang shih shu erh-shih-liu 上歐陽瓣薑師書二十六 [Letter to my teacher Ou-yang Chung-ku, No.

26]
—— CC: pp. 335-337.

September-
October

Ssu-wei i-yün t'ai tuan-shu hsü 思緯壹壹臺短書敍 [Preface to a short discourse from the Ssu-wei i-yün Studio]
—— CC: p. 153.

Ssu-wei i-yün t'ai tuan-shu——pao Pei Yüan-cheng 思緯壹壹臺短書一報貝元徵 [A short discourse from the Ssu-wei i-yün Studio——A letter in reply to Pei Yün-hsin 貝允昕]
—— CC: pp. 389-430.

9 December
(10.23)

Chih Liu Sung-fu shu liu 致劉淞芙書六 [Letter to Liu Shan-han, No. 6]
—— CC: p. 385.

1896 (Kuang-hsü 22nd year. Ping-shen 丙申. Age 32)

2 January
(KH21, 11.18)

Shang Ou-yang Pan-chiang shih shu shih-ssu 上歐陽瓣薑師書十四 [Letter to my teacher Ou-yang Chung-ku, No. 14]
—— CC: pp. 310-311.

4 January
(KH21, 11.20)

Shang Ou-yang Pan-chiang shih shu shih-erh 上歐陽瓣薑師書十二 [Letter to my teacher Ou-yang Chung-ku, No. 12]
—— CC: p. 309.

17 January
(KH21, 12.3)

Shang Ou-yang Pan-chiang shih shu wu 上歐陽瓣薑師書五 [Letter to my teacher Ou-yang Chung-kuo, No. 5]
—— CC: p. 304.

31 January
(KH21, 12.17)

Shang Ou-yang Pan-chiang shih shu shih-i 上歐陽瓣薑師書十一 [Letter to my teacher Ou-yang Chung-ku, No. 11]
—— CC: p. 308.

12 February
(KH21, 12.29)

Shang Ou-yang Pan-chiang shih shu erh-shih-wu 上歐陽瓣薑師書二十五 [Letter to my teacher Ou-yang Chung-ku, No. 25]
—— CC: pp. 332-335.

February
(KH22, 1)

Chih Liu Sung-fu shu liu 致劉淞芙書六 [Letter to Liu Shan-han, No. 6]
—— HN: Vol. 4, pp. 63-64.

7 March
(1.24)

Pao Tsou Yüeh-sheng shu i 報鄒岳生書一 [A letter in reply to Tsou Yüeh-sheng, No. 1]
—— CC: pp. 440-441.

11 March
(1.28)

Shang Ou-yang Pan-chiang shih shu erh-shih-ssu 上歐陽瓣薑師書二十四 [Letter to my teacher Ou-yang Chung-ku, No. 24]
—— CC: pp. 330-332.

Spring   Liu-pieh Hsiang chung t'ung-chih pa p'ien 留別湘中同志八篇
                [Farewell to my friends in Hunan]
                — CC: pp. 483-484.

June   Chih Liu Sung-fu shu erh 致劉淞芙書二 [Letter to Liu
(5)   Shan-han, No. 2]
                — HN: Vol. 4, p. 59.

31 August   Shang Ou-yang Pan-chiang shih shu erh-shih-erh 上歐陽瓣薑
(7.23)   師書二十二 [Letter to my teacher Ou-yang Chung-ku,
                No. 22]
                — CC: pp. 316-328.

October   Chin-ling t'ing shuo-fa san shou 金陵聽說法三首 [Receiving
(9)   instructions on Buddhism in Nanking]
                — CC: p. 485.

Ocotber   Chin-ling t'ing fa shih chu 金陵聽法詩註 [Annotation to
(9)   the poem "Receiving instructions on Buddhism in Nan-
                king"]
                —HN: Vol. 9, pp. 97-98.

October   Sung Wu Yen-chou hsien-sheng kuan Kuei-chou shih hsü
(9)   送吳雁舟先生官貴州詩紋 [Preface to the poem presented
                to Mr. Wu Chia-jui 吳嘉瑞 on his departure to his official
                appointment in Kuei-chou]
                — HN: Vol. 9, p. 98.
                Tseng Wu Yen-chou 贈吳雁舟 [To Wu Chia-jui]
                — CC: p. 479.

October   Pao T'ang Fo-ch'en shu 報唐佛塵書 [A letter in reply to
(9)   T'ang Ts'ai-ch'ang 唐才常]
                — CC: pp. 442-446.

October   Chih Wang K'ang-nien shu i 致汪康年書一 [Letter to Wang
(9)   K'ang-nien, No. 1]
                — CC: pp. 339-340.

27 October   Shang Ou-yang Pan-chiang shih shu erh-shih-san 上歐陽瓣薑
(9.21)   師書二十三 [Letter to my teacher Ou-yang Chung-ku, No. 23]
                — CC: pp. 329-330.

12 November   Pao-chang wen-t'i shuo 報章文體說 [An essay about the
(10.8)   style of newspaper writing]
                — CC: pp. 116-119.
                Tseng Liang Cho-ju ssu shou 贈梁卓如四首 [To Liang Ch'i-
                ch'ao]
                — CC: p. 477.
                Ch'ou Sung Yen-sheng chien-tseng 酬宋燕生見贈 [Re-

sponding to the poem Sung Shu 宋恕 presented to me]
— CC: p. 477.

Fa-jen wu-ku so Tien pien Wu-wu-ti, ching-chieh chih, huo wei chih yao 法人無故索滇邊烏烏地，竟界之，或爲之謠 [A ditty on the French who unreasonably demanded the district of Meng-wu Wu-te 猛烏烏得 in Yunan and even made it their dominion]
— HN: Vol. 9, p. 98.

10 December (11.6)	Shang Ou-yang Pan-chiang shih shu shih-san 上歐陽瓣薑師書十三 [Letter to my teacher Ou-yang Chung-ku, No. 13] — CC: pp. 309-310.
17 December (11.13)	Chih Wang K'ang-nien shu erh 致汪康年書二 [Letter to Wang K'ang-nien, No. 2] — CC: pp. 340-342.
23 December (11.19)	Shang Ou-yang Pan-chiang shih shu chiu 上歐陽瓣薑師書九 [Letter to my teacher Ou-yang Chung-ku, No. 9] — CC: pp. 353-355.

1897 (Kuang-hsü 23rd year. Ting-yu 丁酉 . Age 33)

August 1896- Nov. 1897 (KH22, 7-KH23, 10)	Jen-hsüeh 仁學 [An exposition of benevolence] — CC: pp. 3-90.
11 January (KH22, 12.9)	Yü Liu Shan-han shu 與劉善涵書 [Letter to Liu Shan-han] — *T'an Ssu-t'ung chen-chi*.
20 January (KH22, 12.18)	Shang Chang Hsiao-ta tu-pu chien 上張孝達督部箋 [Letter to the Governor-general Chang Chih-tung 張之洞] — CC: p. 440.
19 February (KH23, 1.18)	Chih Wang K'ang-nien shu san 致汪康年書三 [Letter to Wang K'ang-nien, No. 3) — CC: pp. 342-343.
26 February (1.25)	Shang Ou-yang Pan-chiang shih shu shih-liu 上歐陽瓣薑師書十六 [Letter to my teacher Ou-yang Chung-ku, No. 16] — CC: pp. 312-313.
27 February (1.26)	Chih Wang K'ang-nien shu ssu 致汪康年書四 [Letter to Wang K'ang-nien, No. 4] — CC: pp. 344-346.
February (1)	Kuan-yin piao tzu-hsü 管音表自敍 [Author's preface to "Musical scale for flute"] — HN: Vol. 8, pp. 115-117.

103

9 March
(2.7)

Chih Wang K'ang-nien Liang Ch'i-ch'ao shu erh 致汪康年梁
啓超書二 [Letter to Wang K'ang-nien and Liang Ch'i-ch'ao,
No. 2]
— CC: pp. 371-372.

16 March
(2.14)

Chih Wang K'ang-nien Liang Ch'i-ch'ao shu i 致汪康年梁啓
超書一 [Letter to Wang K'ang-nien and Liang Ch'i-ch'ao,
No. 1]
— CC: pp. 369-371.

18 March
(2.16)

Chih Wang K'ang-nien shu wu 致汪康年書五 [Letter to
Wang K'ang-nien, No. 5]
— CC: pp. 346-349.

27 March
(2.25)

Chih Lung Yü-ch'i shu i 致龍莫溪書一 [Letter to Lung Fu-
jui, No. 1]
— CC: pp. 435-436.

March
(2)

Huang Ying-ch'u "Chuan-ying k'uai-tzu chien-fa" hsü 黃穎初
「傳音快字簡法」敍 [Preface to Huang Ying-ch'u's "A
simple method of shorthand based on pronunciation"]
—HN: Vol. 8, pp. 117-118.

Spring

Liu-yang hsing-suan chi 瀏陽興算記 [A proposal to promote
the learning of mathematics in Liuyang, Hunan]
—HN: Vol. 6, pp. 159-174.

Spring

Chih Lung Yü-ch'i shu ssu 致龍莫溪書四 [Letter to Lung
Fu-jui, No. 4]
— CC: p. 438.

15 April
(3.14)

Chih Liang Ch'i-ch'ao shu 致梁啓超書 [Letter to Liang Ch'i-
ch'ao]
— CC: pp. 373-374.

23 April
(3.22)

Chih Wang K'ang-nien shu ch'i 致汪康年書七 [Letter to
Wang K'ang-nien, No. 7]
— CC: pp. 350-352.

25 April
(3.24)

Chih Wang K'ang-nien shu liu 致汪康年書六 [Letter to Wang
K'ang-nien, No. 6]
— CC: pp. 349-350.

13 May
(4.12)

Chih Lung Yü-ch'i shu wu 致龍莫溪書五 [Letter to Lung
Fu-jui, No. 5]
— CC: p. 438.

May
(4)

Sung Wu Chi-ch'ing Te-su chih kuan Shan-yin 送吳季淸德潚
之官山陰 [To Wu Te-su on his departure to his appoint-
ment at Shan-yin, Chechiang]
— CC: p. 485.

7 June (5.8)	Chih Wang Sung-ku shu i 致汪頌穀書一 [Letter to Wang I-nien 汪詒年 , No. 1] — CC: p. 374.
11 June (5.12)	Chih Wang K'ang-nien shu pa 致汪康年書八 [Letter to Wang K'ang-nien, No. 8] — CC: p. 353.
13 June (5.14)	Chih Wang K'ang-nien shu chiu 致汪康年書九 [Letter to Wang K'ang-nien, No. 9] — CC: pp. 353-355.
16 June (5.17)	Shang Ou-yang Pan-chiang shih shu shih 上歐陽瓣薑師書十 [Letter to my teacher Ou-yang Chung-ku, No. 10] — CC: p. 307.
18 June (5.19)	Chih Wang K'ang-nien shu shih 致汪康年書十 [Letter to Wang K'ang-nien, No. 10] — CC: pp. 355-356.
June (5)	Yü T'ang Fu-ch'eng shu i 與唐紱丞書一 [Letter to T'ang Ts'ai-ch'ang, No. 1] — HN: Vol. 8, pp. 124–126.
June (5)	Ta-hsien Wu-chiao ssu yü Hu-pei, chi fu Chi-ch'ing hsien-sheng chih-hsien Ch'ien-t'ang, yin tsang chu Hsi-hu chih shang, Hsin-hui Liang Ch'i-ch'ao ming chih yüeh "T'ien-min Wu Ch'iao chih mu", Ssu-t'ung chiang wang hui tsang, erh ai i lien-yü 達縣吳樵死於湖北，其父季清先生知縣錢塘，因葬諸西湖之上，新會梁啓超銘之曰，「天民吳樵之墓」，嗣同將往會葬，而哀以聯語 [A couplet to lament, before attending the funeral, Wu Ch'iao of Ta County, Szechuan. Wu died in Hu-pei, but his father, Mr. Wu Te-su 吳德瀟, who is the District Magistrate of Hang-chou, has him buried in the Western Lake. Liang Ch'i-ch'ao of Hsin-hui, Kwangtung, inscribed the words "The Tomb of Wu Ch'iao of Szechuan" on the tombstone] — HN: Vol. 9, p. 100.
June (5)	Mo-ch'ou hu lien-yü 莫愁湖聯語 [A couplet written at Lake Mo-ch'ou] — HN: Vol. 9, p. 100.
June (5)	Wu T'ieh-ch'iao chuan 吳鐵樵傳 [A biography of Wu Ch'iao] — CC: pp. 207-209.
June (5)	Chin-ling ts'e-liang-hui chang-ch'eng 金陵測量會章程 [Regulations of the Nanking Surveying Society] — HN: Vol. 8, pp. 118-120.

29 June (5.30)	Chih Wang K'ang-nien shu shih-i 致汪康年書十一 [Letter to Wang K'ang-nien, No. 11] — CC: pp. 356-357.
4 July (6.5)	Chih Wang K'ang-nien shu shih-erh 致汪康年書十二 [Letter to Wang K'ang-nien, No. 12] — CC: p. 357.
9 July (6.10)	Chih Wang K'ang-nien shu shih-san 致汪康年書十三 [Letter to Wang K'ang-nien, No. 13] — CC: p. 358.
10 July (6.11)	Chih Wang K'ang-nien Liang Ch'i-ch'ao shu san 致汪康年梁啓超書三 [Letter to Wang K'ang-nien and Liang Ch'i-ch'ao, No. 3] — CC: pp. 372-373.
15 July (6.16)	Chih Wang K'ang-nien shu shih-ssu 致汪康年書十四 [Letter to Wang K'ang-nien, No. 14] — CC: pp. 358-359.
23 July (6.24)	Chih Wang K'ang-nien shu shih-wu 致汪康年書十五 [Letter to Wang K'ang-nien, No. 15] — CC: p. 359.
3 August (7.6)	Chih Wang K'ang-nien shu shih-liu 致汪康年書十六 [Letter to Wang K'ang-nien, No. 16] — CC: pp. 360-361.
3 August (7.6)	Chih Wang Sung-ku shu erh 致汪頌穀書二 [Letter to Wang I-nien 汪詒年, No. 2] — CC: p. 375.
7 August (7.10)	Chih Wang K'ang-nien shu shih-ch'i 致汪康年書十七 [Letter to Wang K'ang-nien, No. 17] — CC: p. 361.
August (7)	Yü T'ang Fu-ch'eng shu erh 與唐紱丞書二 [Letter to T'ang Ts'ai-ch'ang, No. 2] — HN: Vol. 8, pp. 126-130.
August (7)	Pao T'u Chih-ch'u shu 報涂質初書 [A letter in reply to T'u Ju-ho 涂儒鬲] — HN: Vol. 8, pp. 135-136.
23 August (7.26)	Chih Wang K'ang-nien shu shih-pa 致汪康年書十八 [Letter to Wang K'ang-nien, No. 18] — CC: pp. 361-362.
August (7)	Ch'uang-pan "K'uang-hsüeh-pao" kung-ch'i 創瓣礦學會公啓 [A public statement concerning the establishment of the *Mining News*] — HN: Vol. 8, pp. 120-122.

6 September (8.10)	Chih Wang K'ang-nien shu shih-chiu 致汪康年書十九 [Letter to Wang K'ang-nien, No. 19] — CC: pp. 362-364.
September (8)	Yü Hsü Yen-fu shu 與徐硯甫書 [A letter to Hsü Jen-chu 徐仁鑄] — HN: Vol. 8, pp. 130-132.
14 September (8.18)	Shang Ou-yang Pan-chiang shih shu pa 上歐陽瓣薑師書八 [Letter to my teacher Ou-yang Chung-ku, No. 8] — CC: pp. 211-212.
25 September (8.29)	Chih Wang K'ang-nien shu erh-shih 致汪康年書二十 [Letter to Wang K'ang-nien, No. 20] — CC: pp. 364-365.
1 October (9.6)	Chih Wang K'ang-nien shu erh-shih-i 致汪康年書二十一 [Letter to Wang K'ang-nien, No. 21] — CC: pp. 365-366.
4 October (9.9)	Chih Lung Yü-ch'i shu san 致龍莫溪書三 [Letter to Lung Fu-jui, No. 3] — CC: p. 437.
5 October (9.10)	Chih Wang K'ang-nien Liang Ch'i-ch'ao shu ssu 致汪康年梁啓超書四 [Letter to Wang K'ang-nien and Liang Ch'i-ch'ao, No. 4] — CC: p. 373.
October (9)	I-mo san-p'ien 遺墨三篇 [Three posthumous poems by T'an Ssu-t'ung] — CC: pp. 280-281.
22 October (9.27)	Chih Wang K'ang-nien shu erh-shih-erh 致汪康年書二十二 [Letter to Wang K'ang-nien, No. 22] — CC: pp. 367-368. Chih Hsü Chi-yü shu 致徐積餘書 [A letter to Hsü Nai-ch'ang 徐乃昌] — CC: p. 446. Chih Liang Ch'i-ch'ao shu 致梁啓超書 [A letter to Liang Ch'i-ch'ao] — *T'an Ssu-t'ung chen-chi.*
12 November (10.18)	Chih Wang K'ang-nien shu erh-shih-san 致汪康年書二十三 [Letter to Wang K'ang-nien, No. 23] — CC: p. 368.
13 November (10.19)	Chih Wang K'ang-nien shu erh-shih-ssu 致汪康年書二十四 [Letter to Wang K'ang-nien, No. 24] — CC: pp. 368-369.

17 November
(10.23)

Shang Ou-yang Pan-chiang shih shu liu 上歐陽瓣薑師書六
[Letter to my teacher Ou-yang Chung-ku, No. 6]
— CC: pp. 304-305.

Ho yu-jen 和友人 [Responding to a friend's poem, using the same rhymes]
— CC: p. 476.

Li yin shih 吏隱詩 [Retiring from office]
— CC: p. 478.

Yu Wu-ch'ang erh Chien-yeh 由武昌而建業 [From Wuchang to Nanking]
— CC: p. 475.

Kuan Chiang-su 官江蘇 [Being an official in Kiangsu]
— CC: p. 487.

Ch'in-huai ho 秦淮河 [River Ch'in-huai]
— CC: p. 488.

Yu kan i chang 有感一章 [An occasional poem]
— CC: p. 488.

Winter

T'i Chiang Chien-hsia "Tung-ling ch'iao hsiao t'u" shih 題江建霞東鄰巧笑圖詩 [Writing a poem on Chiang Piao's 江標 painting, "Charming smiles from the eastern neighbour"]
— HN: Vol. 9, p. 99.

Winter

Sung Chiang Chien-hsia kuei Su-chou shih 送江建霞歸蘇州詩 [Seeing off Chiang Piao on his return to Su-chou]
— HN: Vol. 9, p. 99.

Winter

Ting-yu Chin-ling shih 丁酉金陵詩 [In Nanking, 1897]
— CC: p. 486.

Chü-hua-shih "Ch'iu ying" yen ming 菊花石秋影硯銘 [An inscription on the Ch'iu-ying chrysanthemum-rock inkstone]
— CC: p. 502.

Chü-hua-shih "Shou meng" yen ming 菊花石瘦夢硯銘 [An inscription on the Shou-meng chrysanthemum-rock inkstone]
— CC: p. 502.

Chü-hua-shih "Yao hua" yen ming 菊花石瑤華硯銘 [An inscription on the Yao-hua chrysanthemum-rock inkstone]
— CC: p. 502.

Chü-hua-shih "Kuan lan" yen ming 菊花石觀瀾硯銘 [An inscription on the kuan-lan chrysanthemum-rock inkstone]
— CC: p. 503.

Chü-hua-shih "Chang chiu" yen ming—wei Lung Chao-lin

tso 菊花石長秋硯銘—爲龍爪霖作 [An inscription on the Chang-chiu chrysanthemum-rock inkstone—for Lung Chao-lin]
— CC: p. 503.

Chü-hua-shih yen ming—wei Wu Hsiao-shan tso 菊花石硯銘—爲吳小珊作 [An inscription on a chrysanthemum-rock inkstone—for Wu Hsiao-shan]
— CC: p. 503.

Chü-hua-shih yen ming—wei T'ang Yü-lu tso 菊花石硯銘—爲唐筠廬作 [An inscription on a chrysanthemum-rock inkstone—for T'ang Yü-lu]
—CC: pp. 503-504.

1898 (Kuang-hsü 24th year. Wu-hsü 戊戌 . Age. 34)

January (KH23, 12-KH24, 1)	Shang Ch'en Yu-ming fu-pu shu 上陳右銘撫部書 [A letter to Governor Ch'en Pao-chien 陳寶箴] — HN: Vol. 8, pp. 132-135.
January (KH23, 12-KH24, 1)	Tseng Liang Lien-chien hsien-sheng hsü 贈梁蓮澗先生序 [A preface in prose presented to Mr. Liang Pao-ying 梁寶瑛] — HN: Vol. 8, pp. 137-138.
29 January (KH24, 1.8)	Chih Wang K'ang-nien shu erh-shih-wu 致汪康年書二十五 [Letter to Wang K'ang-nien, No. 25] — CC: p. 369.
10 February (1.20)	Chih Liu Chü-hsing shu erh 致劉聚卿書二 [Letter to Liu Shih-heng 劉世珩, No. 2] — HN: Vol. 9, p. 101.
February (1)	Chih Liu Chü-hsing shu i 致劉聚卿書一 [Letter to Liu Shih-heng, No. 1] —HN: Vol. 9, pp. 100-101.
9 March (2.17)	Lun Chung-kuo ch'ing-hsing wei-chi 論中國情形危急 [On China's critical situation] NOTE: Original title in Vol. 3 of the *Hunan Daily* is "T'an Fu-sheng kuan-ch'a ti-i-tz'u chiang-i" 譚復生觀察第一次講義 [Notes of the first lecture given by Prefect T'an Ssu-t'ung] — CC: pp. 126-128.
10 March (2.18)	Yen-nien-hui hsü 延年會敍 [Preface to the Longevity Society] — CC: pp. 139-144.
14 March (2.22)	Lun chin-jih hsi-hsüeh yü Chung-kuo ku-hsüeh 論今日西學與中國古學 [On present Western learning and ancient Chinese

learning]

NOTE: Original title in Vol. 4 of the *Hunan Daily* is: "T'an Fu-sheng kuan-ch'a Nan-hsüeh-hui ti-erh-tz'u chiang-i" 譚復生觀察南學會第二次講義 [Notes of the second lecture given to the Nan-hsüeh Society by Prefect T'an Ssu-t'ung]

— CC: pp. 128-130.

16 March (2.24)

Shih-hsing yin-hua shui t'iao-shuo 試行印花稅條說 [A proposal to try out a stamp-duty law]

— CC: pp. 121-126.

18 March (2.26)

Hsiang-pao hou-hsü shang 湘報後敘上 [Second preface to the *Hunan Daily*, part 1]

— CC: pp. 136-138.

18 March (2.26)

Hsiang-pao hou-hsü hsia 湘報後敘下 [Second preface to the *Hunan Daily*, part 2]

— CC: pp. 138-139.

18 March (2.26)

Kai-ping Liu-yang ch'eng hsiang ke shu-yüan wei chih-yung hsüeh-t'ang kung-ch'i 改併瀏陽城鄉各書院爲致用學堂公啓 [A public statement regarding a plan to convert academies of the various towns and villages of Liuyang County into schools of practical learning]

— CC: pp. 209-211.

24 March (3.3)

Tu Nan-hai K'ang kung-pu t'iao-ch'en Chiao-shih che shu-hou 讀南海康工部條陳膠事折書後 [Comments on K'ang Yu-wei's memorial on the Chiao-chou Incident]

—HN: Vol. 9, p. 67.

27 March (3.6)

Shang Ou-yang Pan-chiang shih shu erh-shih-ch'i 上歐陽瓣薑師書二十七 [Letter to my teacher Ou-yang Chung-ku, No. 27]

— CC: pp. 337-338.

28 March (3.7)

Lun Hsiang-Yüeh t'ieh-lu chih i 論湘粵鐵路之益 [A discussion of the advantages of a Hunan-Kwangtung Railway]

— CC: pp. 111-116.

March (3)

Chü-hua yen-ming—wei Liang Jen-kung tso 菊花硯銘一爲梁任公作 [An inscription on a chrysanthemum-rock inkstone—for Liang Ch'i-ch'ao]

— CC: p. 501.

29 March (3.8)

Lun hsüeh-che pu-tang chiao-jen 論學者不當驕人 [That scholars ought not to be vain]

NOTE: Original title in Vol. 20 of the *Hunan Daily* is:

"T'an Fu-sheng kuan-ch'a Nan-hsüeh-hui ti-wu-tz'u chiang-i" 譚復生觀察南學會第五次講義 [Notes of the fifth lecture given to the Nan-hsüeh Society by Prefect T'an Ssu-t'ung]
— CC: pp. 130-133.

31 March
(3.10)
Shang Ou-yang Pan-chiang shih shu erh-shih-pa 上歐陽瓣薑師書二十八 [Letter to my teacher Ou-yang Chung-ku, No. 28]
— CC: pp. 338-339.

4 April
(3.14)
Chi kuan-shen chi-i pao-wei-chü shih 記官紳集議保衞局事 [An account of the exchange of opinions between officials and gentry on the establishment of a bureau of local guards]
— CC: pp. 167-168.

8 April
(3.18)
Lun tien-teng chih i 論電燈之益 [A discussion of the advantages of electric light]
— CC: pp. 109-111.

12 April
(3.22)
Ch'ün-meng hsüeh-hui hsü 群萌學會序 [An Introduction to the Ch'ün-meng Study Society]
— CC: pp. 144-148.

15-18 April
(3.25-28)
Chuang-fei lou chih-shih shih p'ien 壯飛樓治事十篇 [Ten essays on statecraft from the Chuang-fei Chamber]
— CC: pp. 91-102.

19 April
(3.29)
Shang Ou-yang Pan-chiang shih·shu shih-wu 上歐陽瓣薑師書十五 [Letter to my teacher Ou-yang Chung-ku, No. 15]
— CC: pp. 311-312.

21 April
(Intercalary 3.1)
Yen-nien-hui kao-pai 延年會告白 [A public notice of the Yen-nien Society]
— *Hsiang-pao*: Vol. 40, p. 160b.

23 April
(Intercalary 3.3)
Lun ch'uan-t'i hsüeh 論全體學 [On human anatomy]
NOTE: Original title in Vol. 23 of the *Hunan Daily* is: "T'an Fu-sheng kuan-ch'a Nan-hsüeh-hui ti-pa-tz'u chiang-i" 譚復生觀察南學會第八次講義 [Notes of the eighth lecture given to the Nan-hsüeh Society by Prefect T'an Ssu-t'ung]
— CC: pp. 133-136.

April-May
(Intercalary 3)
Chih Lung Yü-ch'i shu liu 致龍英溪書六 [Letter to Lung Fu-jui, No. 6]
— CC: pp. 438-439.
Chih Lung Yü-ch'i shu ch'i 致龍英溪書七 [Letter to Lung Fu-jui, No. 7]
— CC: p. 439.

Chih Lung Yü-ch'i shu pa 致龍莫溪書八 [Letter to Lung
Fu-jui, No. 8]
　　— CC: p. 439.

6 May　　Hu-nan pu-ch'an-chü-hui chia-ch'ü chang-ch'eng 湖南不纏足
(Intercalary 3.16)　會嫁娶章程 [Regulations regarding marriage drafted by the
　　　Hunan Non-footbinding Society]
　　— CC: pp. 211-212.

6 May　　I-t'ai shuo 以太說 [An essay on Ether]
(Intercalary 3.16)　　— CC: p. 119.

17 May　　Shang Ou-yang Pan-chiang shih shu shih-pa 上歐陽瓣薑師
(Intercalary 3.27)　書十八 [Letter to my teacher Ou-yang Chung-ku, No. 18]
　　— CC: p. 314.

19 May　　Shang Ou-yang Pan-chiang shih shu shih-chiu 上歐陽瓣薑師
(Intercalary 3.29)　書十九 [Letter to my teacher Ou-yang Chung-ku, No. 19]
　　— CC: pp. 312-315.

20 June　　Chih fu-jen shu 致夫人書 [A letter to my wife]
(5.2)　　— HN: Vol. 3, p. 78.

22 June　　Chih Tsou Yüeh-sheng shu 致鄒岳生書 [A letter to Tsou
(5.4)　　Yüeh-sheng]
　　— HN: Vol. 5, p. 77.

24 June　　Shang Ou-yang Pan-chiang shih shu erh-shih 上歐陽瓣薑師
(5.6)　　書二十 [Letter to my teacher Ou-yang Chung-ku, No. 20]
　　— CC: p. 315.

24 June　　Shang Ou-yang Pan-chiang shih shu san 上歐陽瓣薑師書三
(5.6)　　[Letter to my teacher Ou-yang Chung-ku, No. 3]
　　— CC: pp. 302-303.

24 June　　Shang Ou-yang Pan-chiang shih shu erh-shih-i 上歐陽瓣薑師
(5.6)　　書二十一 [Letter to my teacher Ou-yang Chung-ku, No. 21]
　　— CC: pp. 315-316.

25 June　　Shang Ou-yang Pan-chiang shih shu ssu 上歐陽瓣薑師書四
(5.7)　　[Letter to my teacher Ou-yang Chung-ku, No. 4]
　　— CC: pp. 303-304.

July　　T'i Ch'eng Tzu-ta heng-lan t'u shih 題程子大橫覽圖詩 [A poem
(6)　　on Ch'eng Sung-wan's 程頌萬 panoramic landscape painting]
　　— HN: Vol. 9, p. 99.

　　Wu-hsü pei-shang liu-pieh nei-tzu 戊戌北上留別內子 [Parting
　　with my wife in 1898 for the North]
　　— CC: p. 495.

31 July　　Chih fu-jen shu i 致夫人書一 [Letter to my wife, No. 1]
(6.13)　　— HN: Vol. 5, p. 76.

27 August   Chih fu-jen shu erh 致夫人書二 [Letter to my wife, No. 2]
(7.11)   — HN: Vol. 5, pp. 76-77.

24 September Yü-chung i-cha san 獄中遺扎三 [Prison letters, No. 3]
·(8.9)   — CC: p. 447.

25 September Yü-chung i-cha i 獄中遺扎一 [Prison letters, No. 1]
(8.10)   — CC: p. 447.

25 September Yü-chung t'i-pi 獄中題壁 [Poem written on the prison wall]
(8.10)   — CC: p. 496.

26 September Yü-chung i-cha erh 獄中遺扎二 [Prison letters, No. 2]
(8.11)   — CC: pp. 447-448.

28 September Lin-chung yü 臨終語 [Words before execution]
(8.13)   — CC: p. 512.

Works of Uncertain Dates

Teng Hung-shan Pao-t'ung-ssu t'a 登洪山寶通寺塔 [Mounting the Pao-t'ung Temple Tower at Mount Hung]
    — CC: pp. 458-459.

Kuai-shih ko 怪石歌 [Song of irregularly-shaped rocks]
    — CC: pp. 460-461.

Ying-wu chou tiao Mi Cheng-p'ing 鸚鵡洲弔禰正平 [Mourning Mi Heng 禰衡 at Ying-wu chou]
    — CC: p. 463.

Chiang shang wen ti shih feng huai Ch'en I-ning kung lien ju chien-chao ching pu tzu-pa 江上聞笛詩奉懷陳義寧公連辱見招竟不自拔 [Remembering, upon hearing the sound of a flute on a river, the revered Mr. Ch'en Pao-chen 陳寶箴 who condescended to ask for my assistance several times to which request regrettably I did not respond]
    — CC: p. 465.

Han shang chi-shih ssu p'ien 漢上紀事四篇 [Events on the River Han]
    — CC: p. 470.

Ch'en teng Heng-yüeh Chu-jung feng erh p'ien 晨登衡嶽祝融峯二篇 [Climbing up Peak Chu-jung of the Heng Mountain in the morning]
    — CC: p. 471.

Lung-shan tao chung 隴山道中 [On a track in Mount Lung, Shensi]
    — CC: p. 472.

Shan chü 山居 [Living in a mountain]
    — CC: p. 472.

Feng-chiang-ch'iao hsiao fa 楓槳橋曉發 [Starting a journey from the Feng-

chiang Bridge at dawn]
— CC: p. 472.

Ch'iu je 秋熱 [The heat of Autumn]
— CC: p. 473.

Kuei hua 桂花 [Sweet osmanthus]
— CC: p. 473.

Ch'in-ling Han Wen-kung ts'u 秦嶺韓文公祠 [The shrine of Han Yü at Ch'in-ling]
— CC: p. 474.

Hsiang shui 湘水 [River Hsiang]
— CC: p. 474.

Yüeh-yang lou 岳陽樓 [The Yüeh-yang Tower]
— CC: p. 474.

Tseng wu-jen shih 贈舞人詩 [To a swordsman]
— CC: p. 476.

Tsu feng Tung-t'ing-hu tseng Li chün Shih-min 阻風洞庭湖贈李君時敏 [To Mr. Lee Shih-min while detained by gust at Lake Tungt'ing]
— CC: p. 478.

Yeh ch'eng 夜城 [The town at night]
— CC: p. 479.

Lan Wu-han hsing-shih 覽武漢形勢 [Taking a look at the topography of Wu-chang and Hankou]
— CC: p. 481.

Kan-huai ssu p'ien 感懷四篇 [Feelings]
— CC: p. 484.

Tzu-t'i shan-shui hua shan 自題山水畫扇 [Writing a poem on my landscape fan-painting]
— CC: p. 486.

Huai-yin-hou mu 淮陰侯墓 [The grave of Han Hsin 韓信]
— CC: p. 486.

Chi jen 寄人 [To a friend]
— CC: p. 486.

Ch'iu hai-t'ang 秋海棠 [Begonia]
— CC: p. 487.

Hua lan 畫蘭 [Painting an orchid]
— CC: p. 489.

Shan-hsi tao-chung erh p'ien 陝西道中二篇 [Travelling in Shensi]
— CC: p. 489.

Tung-t'ing tsu feng 洞庭阻風 [Detained by gust at Lake Tungt'ing]
— CC: p. 491.

Tao p'ang liu 道旁柳 [Roadside willow]
— CC: p. 492.

Pin-chou 邠州 [Pinchou in Shensi]
— CC: p. 492.

Ma ming 馬鳴 [Neigh]
— CC: p. 492.

Mu-tan fo-shou hua chang 牡丹佛手畫障 [A screen with the painting of peony and fingered citron]
— CC: p. 493.

Kan-su pu-cheng-shih-shu   Ch'i-yüan ch'iu-jih 甘肅布政使署憩園秋日 [An autumn day at Garden Rest of the Kansu Under-Governor's official lodging]
— CC: p. 493.

Chiang-hsing kan-chiu shih ai wai-chiu chia yeh 江行感舊詩哀外舅家也 [Mourning my father-in-law while recollecting past events on a river tour]
— CC: p. 494.

T'i Ts'an-hsüeh chin ming 題殘雪琴銘 [Writing an inscription on the Ts'an-hsüeh lute]
— CC: p. 501.

Tsou yen ming ping hsü 鄒硯銘幷敍 [An inscription on Tsou (Yüeh-sheng's 岳生) inkstone, with preface]
— CC: p. 504.

T'ing-yün chin ming—wei Li Jen-sheng tso 停雲琴銘一爲黎壬生作 [An inscription on the T'ing-yün lute, for Li Jen-sheng]
— CC: p. 504.

Tan-tao ming ping hsü 單刀銘並敍 [On single broadsword, with preface]
— CC: p. 504.

Shuang-chien ming 雙劍銘 [On a pair of swords]
— CC: p. 504.

Ch'an ting ming 讒鼎銘 [On the "Ch'an" tripod]
— CC: p. 505.

Fu Pao Kao-wen hsiao-chao tsan ping hsü 傅保高媼小照贊幷敍 [A eulogy on a small photograph of Mrs. Kao, nanny and tutor, with preface]
— CC: p. 505.

Hsiao Yüan-hsüan hsiang tsan 蕭箑軒像贊 [A eulogy on a portrait of Hsiao Yüan-hsüan]
— CC: p. 506.

Hua hsiang tsan 畫像贊 [A eulogy on a portrait (of Li Ch'ang-chi 李長吉)]
— CC: p. 507.

P'eng Yün-fei hsiang tsan 彭雲飛像贊 [A eulogy on a portrait of P'eng Yün-fei]
— CC: p. 507.

115

T'i hsien chung-hsiung mu chien shih-chu 題先仲兄墓前石柱 [Writing a couplet on a stone column in front of my late elder brother's grave]
— CC: p. 509.

Wan Liu Hsiang-ch'in kung 輓劉襄勤公 [Mourning the late Mr. Liu Chin-t'ang 劉錦棠]
— CC: p. 509.

Tseng Liu Sung-fu 贈劉淞芙 [To Liu Shan-han 劉善涵]
— CC: p. 509.

Tseng Huang Ying-ch'u 贈黃穎初 [To Huang Ying-ch'u]
— CC: p. 510.

Hsi t'ai 戲台 [Theatre stage]
— CC: p. 510.

Tseng mou yu-jen 贈某友人 [To a certain friend]
— CC: p. 510.

Chi tz'u t'i Ch'in-huai hua-fang 集詞題秦淮畫舫 [On Ch'in-huai Pleasure-boat, a *tz'u* made up of lines from various *tz'u* composers]
— CC: p. 510.

Chi Hua-yen t'i Ch'in-huai shui-hsieh 集華嚴題秦淮水榭 [On Ch'in-huai Pavilion, a couplet made up of lines from the *Garland Sutra*]
— CC: p. 511.

Chi-chiu p'ien 急就篇 [An impromptu]
— CC: p. 511.

Tseng mou yu-jen 贈某友人 [To a certain friend]
— CC: p. 511.

Tseng mou yu-jen 贈某友人 [To a certain friend]
— CC: p. 511.

Ke-yen 格言 [A maxim]
— CC: p. 512.

Jih sung 日頌 [My daily schedule]
— CC: p. 512.

Chang-tzu Cheng-meng-ts'an liang p'ien pu-chu 張子正蒙參兩篇補註 [Supplementary annotations to "A textual examination of Chang Tsai's *Cheng-meng*"]
— see CC: p. 205.

T'i Ku Shih-kung so pien Ku-shih chung-chen lu chien ta ch'i chien-tseng shih 題顧石公所編顧氏忠貞錄兼答其見贈詩 [Writing a poem on *A Family History of the Kus*, edited by Ku Yün 顧雲 , as a reply to the poem he presented to me]
— HN: Vol. 9, p. 98.

Chi T'ang Fu-ch'eng shih 寄唐紱丞詩 [A poem to T'ang Ts'ai-ch'ang]
— HN: Vol. 9, p. 98.

116

Chi ti Ch'in-sheng shih 寄弟秦生詩 [A poem to my younger brother T'an Ssu-chiung 譚嗣岡]
— HN: Vol. 9, p. 99.

Writings of Dubious Authorship

Pao Tsou Yüeh-sheng shu erh 報鄒岳生書二 [A letter in reply to Tsou Yüeh-sheng, No. 2]
— CC: p. 441.
Tseng Ch'iu Wen-chieh 贈邱文階 [To Ch'iu Wen-chieh]
— CC: p. 475.
Shu huai 述懷 [My feelings]
— CC: p. 451.